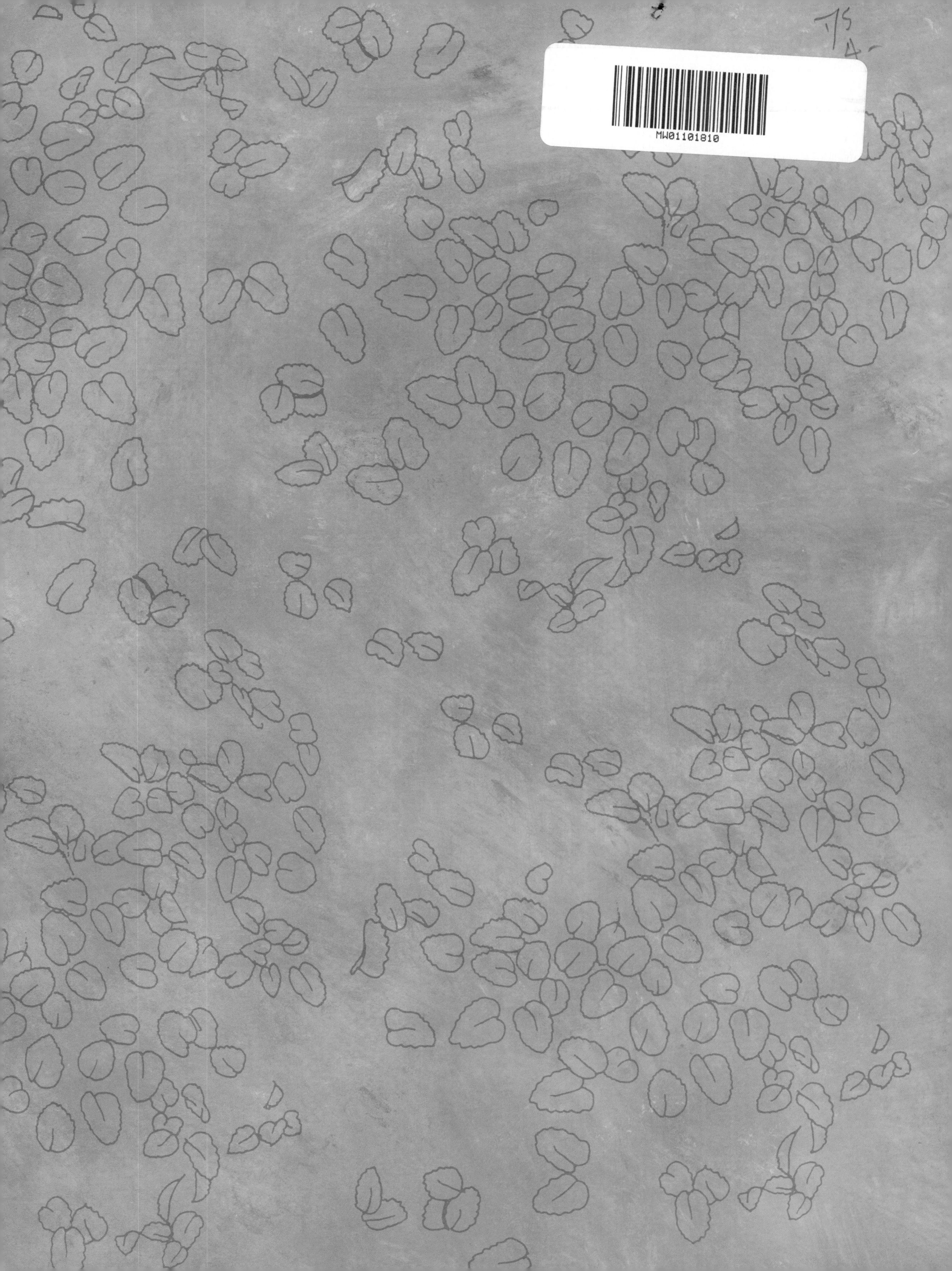

TASMANIA'S HERITAGE

An Enduring Legacy

ESK VIEW
TERRACE

TASMANIA'S HERITAGE

An Enduring Legacy

Jennifer Pringle-Jones
Ray Joyce

ST DAVID'S PARK PUBLISHING
2 SALAMANCA PLACE, HOBART, TASMANIA, AUSTRALIA 7000
FIRST PUBLISHED 1991

Designed by Brita Hansen

The author gratefully acknowledges the assistance of officers from the following organisations, centres and government departments:

Allport Library and Museum of Fine Arts
Australian Heritage Commission
Launceston Maritime Museum
National Trust of Australia (Tasmania)
Port Arthur Historic Site Management Authority
Queen Victoria Museum and Art Gallery
Register of the National Estate
Tasmaniana Library
Tasmanian Aboriginal Land Council
Tasmanian Forestry Commission
Tasmanian Office of Aboriginal Affairs
Tasmanian Chamber of Mines
Tasmanian Department of Parks, Wildlife and Heritage
Tasmanian Department of Primary Industry
Tasmanian Museum and Art Gallery
Tourism Tasmania
The Wilderness Society
University of Tasmania School of Design

NATIONAL LIBRARY OF AUSTRALIA
CATALOGUING-IN-PUBLICATION DATA:

Pringle-Jones, Jennifer, 1946-
TASMANIA'S HERITAGE An Enduring Legacy

ISBN 0 7246 2161X

1. Tasmania — History. 2. Tasmania — Description and Travel — 1990-. I. Title
994.6

Printed in Tasmania by:
TASMANIAN GOVERNMENT PRINTING OFFICE

Contents

Title pages: Rural advertising, Tunbridge

Esk View Terrace, Launceston

Government House, Hobart

FOREWORD

By
His Excellency General Sir Phillip Bennett, A.C., K.B.E., D.S.O.
Governor of Tasmania

Tasmania is renowned as one of the most beautiful islands in the world. This is because our natural beauty, manifested in scenic lakes, imposing mountains and unspoiled beaches, is successfully married with our man-made heritage of grand buildings, majestic bridges and charming villages.

Tasmania also has less immediately quantifiable assets - clean water, an unhurried lifestyle, specialist industries and crafts and an appreciation of those particular attributes.

In this book, Ray Joyce and Jennifer Pringle-Jones have given us an excellent insight into the State, with a compehensive and well-researched text, and with many illustrations showing the splendour of Tasmania.

The book traces the growth of the State through settlement, early exploration, and modern-day developments in business, sport and the arts. It is especially appropriate that the wealth of Tasmania's architectural heritage receives significant attention both in the commentary and in the photographs.

I commend this project, and also St David's Park Publishing, an imprint of the Tasmanian Government Printing Office, for ensuring that as far as possible this is a truly Tasmanian publication.

I know that **TASMANIA'S HERITAGE An Enduring Legacy** is an accurate reflection of why we who live here love this island, and I am confident that it will also stand as a lasting memento for visitors to Tasmania.

GOVERNOR

▲
The multiple Liffey Falls cascade through rainforest in the Liffey Valley

◀
Hastings Caves in southern Tasmania consist of three limestone caves, the largest of which is Newdegate Cave

Australia's island state of Tasmania is not large but about 20% of its 68,000 square-kilometre area is considered to be of such outstanding universal value that it has been included on UNESCO's World Heritage List, established by the World Heritage Convention.

The Tasmanian Wilderness World Heritage Area, which covers approximately 1.383 million hectares of western, south-western and central regions, ranks alongside more than 300 other listed properties such as the Grand Canyon National Park, Westminster Abbey, the Taj Mahal and the Great Barrier Reef as significant cultural or national treasures. Their protection is considered to be in the interest of all nations.

In Tasmania, the World Heritage Area provides a notable example of a major stage of the earth's evolutionary history, with evidence of ongoing geological processes and biological evolution. It is also the most important natural habitat for a number of threatened species of plants and animals that are of international scientific interest, along with the area's rich Aboriginal archaeological sites of Ice Age and more recent origin.

In addition to the World Heritage listing, Tasmania has more than 1,300 places on Australia's Register of the National Estate. Prepared by the Australian Heritage Commission, a statutory body of the Commonwealth Government, the register includes elements of the natural and built environment that have "aesthetic, historic, scientific or cultural significance, or other special value" for present and future generations. National parks and nature reserves, caves and other geological features, shipwrecks, historic towns, notable buildings, engineering works and Aboriginal sites are among the listings.

Contributors to the register include Commonwealth and State governments, the Australian Institute of Aboriginal Studies, universities, the National Trust of Australia and nature conservation groups.

One of the aims of the National Estate is to increase the respect of white Australians for the culture of the first inhabitants of this country while, at the same time, creating a greater awareness of the heritage that stems from the early days of settlement by Europeans after 1788.

National Estate grants from the Australian Heritage Commission are among those that have contributed to archaeological surveys and research of Aboriginal sites in Tasmania, especially in the South and South-West. Ongoing investigations at open campsites marked by scatters of stone tools, in caves and rockshelters are helping to build up a picture of the lifestyle and culture of Aborigines in the past, with evidence of occupation in some shelters of inland southern and western Tasmania between at least 31,000 and 10,000 years ago.

The Aborigines travelled to Tasmania from mainland Australia when a land bridge existed before the flooding of Bass Strait, the stretch of water that carried many of the latter-day explorers and settlers of the island.

Legacies built up over thousands of years, coupled with natural splendour, have endowed Tasmania with a rich heritage that has to be seen to be appreciated. This book is intended to provide an insight into the geography, fauna, flora, buildings, monuments, ruins and other structures that contribute to this heritage.

Heritage of Nature

Tasmania is among the world's oldest lands with rock formations such as the central south-west mountain ranges dating back 700-1,000 million years. It is a particularly mountainous island, especially in the western half, which includes coastal platforms, ranges and a high dissected plateau. The north-west plateau, the Tamar rift-valley and the north-east coastal platform run along the north coast and continue inland for about 30 kilometres. A central plateau, which often rises to more than 900 metres, is south of the north-west plateau. This central plateau is sometimes referred to as the Land of a Thousand Lakes, but the total number of lakes and tarns is actually about 3,000. The north-east highlands and Ben Lomond Horst, which consist mainly of uplifted remnants of old fold mountains, are south of the north-east coastal platform. A low-dissected platform in the South-East includes the Tasman and Forestier Peninsulas and the drowned estuary of the River Derwent in the extreme South. Tasmania's South-West, the Southern Alps-Fiordland region of New Zealand and the Patagonian Andes in South America are the last three great temperate wilderness areas in the southern hemisphere.

◀
River Derwent near New Norfolk

▲▲
Fern glen in World Heritage Area near Nelson Falls

▲
Mount Wellington (Tasmaniana Library collection)

◀◀ *Pandani, a member of the heath family*

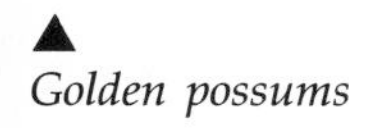

▲ *Golden possums*

◀ *Fungi*

◀ *Alpine moors*

▲
Granite peaks of The Hazards at Coles Bay

Among the more evocative mountains are Frenchmans Cap (1443m), a white, shiny peak of quartzite rock named by explorers who said it resembled the caps worn by Frenchmen in the early 19th century, Cradle Mountain, the rugged granite peaks of the Strzelecki Range on Flinders Island and dolerite-capped Mt Ossa, which at 1617m is the highest mountain in the State. The Hartz Mountains, set amidst alpine moorlands dotted with picturesque lakes, Ben Lomond, the only part of north-eastern Tasmania affected by glaciers, and Mt Wellington, which towers 1271m above the capital city, Hobart, have also drawn admirers for centuries.

Mt Wellington, which was known as Table Mountain by early European settlers because it reminded them of South Africa's mountain of that name, was described by author, poet and naturalist Louisa Anne Meredith in her book, "My Home in Van Diemen's Land during a residence of 9 years", published in 1852:

"Whether it was wreathed in fleecy vapours, dark with rolling clouds, or stood out clear and sunlit against the blue morning sky, I was never weary of gazing on this magnificent object. Its aspect is one of ever-varying but never-decreasing grandeur."

With her husband, Charles, Mrs Meredith was a pioneer of the east coast, a feature of which is the Schouten Range. These formations also provided her with literary inspiration...

"The mountainous chain or group of the Schoutens is most picturesquely composed; the mainland portion commences next to the mouth of Swan Port, in three chief eminences, running nearly parallel east and west; these are connected by a narrow isthmus of lowland running from the western side, with another group of sublime bare granite peaks, trending to the south, and between which and the triple mount, the bright blue waves of the Pacific flow into 'Wineglass Bay' ('Thouin's Bay' of the published maps). A strait called the 'Schouten Passage' separates three kindred crags from the Schouten Island, which stretches still farther south, its swelling heights and almost inaccessible rocky ranges crowned by a lofty dome-shaped mount, and its southern extremity ending in an abrupt precipitous bluff."

Winter in the Hartz Mountains National Park

Others: Flowerings of the bush

▶▶
Dove Lake at the northern end of the Cradle Mountain-Lake St Clair National Park

Fossil Bluff, north-west coast, where one of Australia's oldest fossil marsupials was found

▶▶ *Cape Raoul, a dominant coastal landmark*

▶▶ *Cape Pillar (Tasmaniana Library collection)*

Other coastal landmarks that have attracted writers, artists and photographers over the years include Cape Raoul and Cape Pillar in the South-East. According to "A Statistical View of Van Diemen's Land 1831, compiled from the most authoritative sources", Cape Raoul has the *"singular appearance of a stupendous Gothic ruin, projecting abruptly into the ocean, with its massive pillars rising up in the manner of minarets or turrets with the tremendous waves dashing against its dark and rugged walls below."* (Later, parts of the rock formation were partially destroyed when they were used for target practice by the British Navy.)

Cape Pillar was reported to have *"basaltic columns, built up as it were to an enormous height, and from the regularity with which they are raised or piled, would almost seem to have been effected by human hands."*

Until the 1980s, the best-known rivers in this State were the Derwent, which traverses the island from Lake St Clair in the West to Storm Bay in the South, the Tamar, which flows to Bass Strait from the site of Australia's third oldest city, Launceston, and the Gordon, in western Tasmania. This changed, however, when international attention focussed on the island as a result of conflict centred on the future of the Franklin River in the West. Developers wanting to dam this essentially wild river for hydro-electric power were opposed by conservationists seeking retention of the river in its natural state, plus that of associated features including caves with evidence of Ice Age Aboriginal occupation and some of the world's oldest rock art.

The conservationists were successful in their bid and the river is now included in the World Heritage Area.

Tasmania was once part of the ancient continent of Gondwana, together with the rest of Australia, India, Antarctica, parts of Africa and South America. This supercontinent broke apart more than 55 million years ago, but Tasmania still has a number of plant and animal species derived from those of Gondwanaland, especially in the cool, temperate rainforests and alpine areas.

The island's fauna and flora is of world importance because there is a high proportion of endemic species and relict groups of ancient lineage. Gondwanan conifers of the alpine moorlands and rainforests are only found in this island, while marsupials, burrowing freshwater crayfish, the Tasmanian cave spider and mountain shrimp also have Gondwanan affinities.

The distribution of several mammals that were once widespread in Australia is now limited to Tasmania. The Tasmanian devil, so-named by European settlers because of its spine-chilling screeches, black colour and reputed bad temper, has powerful jaws and teeth that enable it to completely devour its prey.

J.S. Prout

The devils were a nuisance in the early days of town settlement because of their raids on poultry yards. Farmers, too, had to contend with the problem, prompting the Van Diemen's Land Company, which opened up the far North-West, to introduce a bounty scheme in 1830. In present-day terms, this scheme has proved more successful in eliminating its other target - the thylacine, commonly known as the Tasmanian tiger or marsupial wolf.

By 1941, when the devils were declared a legally protected species, they had become quite rare. However, their numbers have now increased again - unlike the Tasmanian tiger.

Despite many searches, there have been no authenticated sightings of the tiger since the last captured specimen died in the Hobart Zoo in 1936.

While farmers no longer need fear the tiger, the animals were an obvious threat in the 1820s when Surveyor-General George William Evans wrote the following excerpt in his book, "A geographical, historical and topographical Description of Van Diemen's Land with important hints to emigrants"...

"There is an animal of the panther tribe which, though not found in such numbers as the native dog is in New Holland, commits dreadful havoc among the flocks. It is true the ravages are not so frequent; but, when they happen, they are more extensive. This animal is of considerable size, and has been known, in a few instances, to measure six feet and a half from the tip of the nose to the extremity of the tail. Still it is cowardly, and by no means formidable to man: indeed, unless when taken by surprize, it invariably flees from his approach."

▲▲
Tasmanian tiger

▲
Tasmanian devil

◀▲
Denison Beach Rivulet

◀
Apsley Gorge, a feature of the Douglas-Apsley National Park

Another endangered species is the orange-bellied parrot, but, as a result of efforts by staff of the Department of Parks, Wildlife and Heritage, the number of parrots is now increasing. It is even possible to view the birds from a specially constructed birdhide at Melaleuca, near Port Davey, in the South-West. Orange-bellied parrots, which are one of Australia's rarest birds, only breed in south-western Tasmania. During winter, they migrate to coastal Victoria and South Australia, returning to Tasmania in September-October.

The wildlife departments of the Commonwealth Government and the State governments of Tasmania, South Australia and Victoria joined forces in the 1980s to form an Orange-bellied Parrot Recovery Team. They have been assisted by the Royal Australasian Ornithologists' Union and the World Wildlife Fund (Australia). In addition to monitoring and managing the birds' natural habitats, the team has succesfully bred orange-bellied parrots in captivity.

The insularity of Tasmania has contributed to the uniqueness of its flora and fauna, the isolation having helped to protect it against the impact of exotic species, such as foxes, which have adversely affected fauna on parts of mainland Australia- including migrating orange-bellied parrots. Offshore islands in Bass Strait, notably the Furneaux Group, are the main habitat of short-tailed shearwaters, commonly called muttonbirds. Each year these remarkable birds fly about 30,000 kilometres from their breeding grounds on the islands, heading north via Japan and the Aleutian islands and on to Alaska. About six months later they return and make their way to the burrow of their birth. To Aborigines, the birds known as "Yolla" are not only a traditional food, but also an important industry. At the annual "birding time", many families return to offshore islands - maintaining an unbroken tradition stretching back over 200 generations.

Cape Barren geese, which are regarded as the second rarest goose species, are concentrated in larger numbers on the islands of the Furneaux group than anywhere else. Special sanctuaries for these handsome, grey birds have been established on Flinders Island.

Some animals, trees and plants remained in Tasmania when the world's ice cap thawed about 11,000 years ago and the 140-kilometre stretch of water, now known as Bass Strait, divided Tasmanian islands from mainland Australia. Trees of the gnarled Banksia serrata, for instance, have continued to thrive at Sisters Beach on the north-west coast, while the slow-growing, durable Huon pine, so-prized by boatbuilders of the past and craftspeople of the present, is found only in Tasmania.

Huon pine was discovered by the Reverend Robert Knopwood, the colony's first chaplain, during a trip up the Huon River in 1804, but it was the stands in the Port Davey area and along west coast rivers like the Gordon River that attracted the majority of "prospectors" seeking this "green gold." During an archaeological study of the

▲▲
Lake Dulverton, Oatlands, is among the State's wildlife sanctuaries

▲
Muttonbirds in flight off Badger Island (Tasmaniana Library collection)

◀
Myrtle forest in World Heritage Area

▶
Gordon River

▼
Leatherwood flowers,contributors to the honey industry

Gordon in the 1980s, a total of 28 sites associated with 19th and early 20th century Huon pining were recorded. They ranged from bush timber mills to temporary camp huts, all of which are remnants of an industry that is never likely to be revived because of resource and access limitations.

It takes up to 800 years for Huon pine to grow to 60cm in diameter, with some specimens being at least 2,000 years old. A remnant stand of 1,000-year-old Huon pines can be seen on the Denison River, in the Wild Rivers National Park of south-western Tasmania. These unique trees are only found in the rainforests of the West, generally below the Pieman River, and in the South. Huon pine is not scarce but its availability is limited as 95% occurs in World Heritage Areas or national parks. Other species in Tasmania's cool temperate rainforests, which cover about 11% of the island, include myrtle, sassafras, leatherwood, celery-top pine, King Billy pine and pencil pine.

The leatherwood tree is a valuable contributor to Tasmania's honey industry, beekeepers leaving their hives by the trees when the white, waxy flowers appear between December and March. The unique leatherwood honey isn't the only product of these trees, though. Colonial explorers called them salvewood as they found that a sticky substance that adheres to the young growth proved useful in healing cuts.

Sassafras has also served a number of purposes for mankind. It was a popular source of home brew for new settlers and in the heyday of wooden clothes pegs it was readily utilised for production in a peg factory at New Norfolk!

Travellers of the early 19th century were among the first to note the beauty of the myrtle forests of the North-West. In the Hobart Town Almanack and Van Diemen's Land Annual of 1830, Government Printer James Ross gave an account of his experience. He said the trees were *"tall and stately - like an English elm or holm."* He went on to say they were *"interspersed with numerous gigantic fern trees, which with their palm like umbrella tops to the height of 20 or 30 feet, afforded the most romantic and agreeable shade to the travellers.*

The moisture and vegetation is so great, and the soil is so rich, that there appears a struggle among the several species for space wherein to grow. Frequently may be seen three or four plants springing from the same root."

The largest areas of rainforest are in the North-West, with fire - the major destroyer of rainforest - limiting its development in places like the South-West, which is burnt more frequently. Killy Billy pines, which are related to the Californian Redwoods, are particularly vulnerable if fires occur because they generally do not regenerate after burning. Blackwood is commonly found where rainforest has been disturbed, especially by fires.

▶▶
Rainforest walk on Sarah Island, Macquarie Harbour

The Tasmanian Department of Parks, Wildlife and Heritage and the Forestry Commission have developed five sites to help visitors better understand and appreciate rainforests. They are at Julius River (near Smithton), Sandspit River (near Orford), by the Lake Pedder Road, at Weldborough Pass (north-west of St Helens), and south of Queenstown at Newall Creek (on the Mt Jukes Road). In many instances, organisations and companies with an interest in these areas have assisted in the establishment of the reserves.

Tasmania is a participant in the National Rainforest Conservation Program, which is enhancing the understanding of rainforests and providing the basic knowledge necessary for long-term conservation.

This State has frequently led the way in Australia in the conservation of areas of natural heritage. A reserve was established at Russell Falls, now in the Mt Field National Park, as early as 1885, and the merits of the lower Gordon River were officially recognised in 1908 when this, too, was set aside as a reserve.

The introduction of a "Scenery Preservation Act" in 1915 was the first legislation of its kind in Australia, with subsequent declaration of reserves, including national parks.

One of the areas to be gazetted more recently under the Forestry Act is the Evercreech Forest Reserve near Fingal. Classified as a wet forest gully, this contains the tallest white gum in the world. Standing 89 metres and with a girth of more than 10 metres, it is the main focus of a group of white gums that have become part of the National Estate and are classified by the National Trust on its register of significant trees.

These gums are survivors in more ways than one. When the area was selectively logged in the 1940s and 50s the common method of extraction was bullock teams, but the larger trees won a reprieve because they were generally impossible to handle this way. The merit of the trees was recognised by foresters during subsequent mechanised logging and, as a result, the gums still stand as a testimony to endurance.

The success of Tasmania's overall conservation movement is due, in part, to the education and lobbying of groups like the Tasmanian Fauna and Flora Conservation Committee, which was followed by the Tasmanian Wilderness Society and the Tasmanian Conservation Trust.

Momentum gathered in the 1960s when conflict centred on the construction of a hydro-electricity scheme that eventually inundated Lake Pedder, an inland lake that was the main feature of the Lake Pedder National Park. The Commonwealth Government later resolved to meet the costs entailed in modifying the scheme to save the lake, but this was not accepted by the State Government and the scheme proceeded.

Proposals for another hydro development on the lower Gordon River downstream of its confluence with the Franklin River aroused more public controversy in the early 1980s. Debate continued between individuals, two successive State governments, the Commonwealth Government and, finally, the High Court of Australia, which upheld the power of the Commonwealth to prevent a dam being built in a World Heritage Area.

◀◀
Pencil pines at Little Pine Lagoon, Central Highlands

◀
Tessellated pavement, Eaglehawk Neck, where cracked mudstone creates the appearance of paving stones

▼
Sand dunes at Seymour on the east coast

▼▼
Franklin River (Photo: Tourism Tasmania)

Settlement

▲
Petroglyphs at Mount Cameron West and Sundown Point on the north-west coast (From the Department of Parks, Wildlife and Heritage Aboriginal Site Register)

◀
Oyster Cove, a sacred Aboriginal site

The evidence of human occupation in Tasmania dates back at least 30,000 years - well before the last Ice Age, which began 25,000 years ago. At that time, Tasmanian Aborigines were the earth's most southerly human inhabitants.

They lived in caves and rock shelters, many of which still contain bones, including those of the animals and birds that were hunted, and bone tools, as well as stone flakes and tools.

About 80 Ice Age Aboriginal rock shelters have been found in southern and western Tasmania, Kutikina and Deena Reena caves on the lower Franklin River yielding particularly rich remnants of pre-historic habitation. A few tools recovered from Kutikina were made from glassy material derived from a large meteorite crater about 25 kilometres north-west of the cave. Known as Darwin glass, it was very good for tool-making because it produced a sharp cutting edge when flaked.

Researchers have also found three other caves with significant hand stencils and ochre smears that demonstrate the artistic side of Tasmanian culture in the Ice Age. They are Wargata Mina in the Cracroft Valley, Ballawinne Cave in the Maxwell Valley and Keyhole Cavern in the Weld Valley. One example of this art is more than 10,000 years old, making it among the world's earliest dated art.

These sites are of great educational and spiritual significance to today's Aboriginal community, whose ancestors lived and painted in the caves, and the State Government has plans to vest the ownership and control of the sites with the Tasmanian Aboriginal Land Council. The Tasmanian Aboriginal community is also seeking the official return of a number of other places that form the central focus of Aboriginal culture. These include Wybalenna, on Flinders Island, where many survivors of the Aboriginal population were taken to live in the 1830s and 1840s, Oyster Cove, where famous Aborigine Truganini (also known as Lalla Rookh) lived before moving to Hobart, where she died in 1876, the main muttonbird islands of Bass Strait, and the Bay of Fires, named in 1773 by British explorer Captain Tobias Furneaux when he saw Aborigines' fires on the east coast.

▲
"Aborigines of Tasmania", painted in 1859 by colonial artist Robert Dowling, with figures based on portraits by Thomas Bock (From the collection of the Queen Victoria Museum and Art Gallery)

▶
Hand stencils at the Wargata Mina Aboriginal site in the Cracroft Valley (From the Department of Parks, Wildlife and Heritage Aboriginal Site Register)

The Aborigines have a close spiritual and cultural affinity with the sea. They once hunted seals and still enjoy muttonbirds and many varieties of shellfish. Although evidence of their occupation along the coast during the Ice Age disappeared when sea levels rose after the end of this period it is known that Tasmanian Aborigines started to use the present coastline about 3,000 years ago. There are signs right around the coast, especially in the middens of the west coast.

Some aspects of Aboriginal heritage are still a puzzle. Aborigines built stone fish traps at Rocky Cape and Port Arthur but some time after this an unexplained taboo was placed on eating scale fish - a taboo that was still observed when contact was made with Europeans. Likewise, investigators have been unable, to date, to comprehend the significance of an ancient layered ceremonial stone arrangement near the Bay of Fires and rock formations at Falmouth and Forcett.

Internationally renowned researcher Dr Rhys Jones, the Senior Fellow in the Department of Prehistory at the Australian National University, claims that north-western Tasmania has one of the most complete archaeological resource bases for the investigation of the history of a coastal hunting and gathering society.

Rock art and other remains of Aboriginal habitation on the west and north-west coasts, and on off-shore island such as Hunter Island in Bass Strait, have been the subject of intense scientific study. Hearths, shell middens, quartz flakes and faunal remains, some of which date back about 22,000 years, have been found in Cave Bay on Hunter Island. South Cave and North Cave at Rocky Cape, on the north-west coast, also contain abundant evidence of Aboriginal occupation, notably in the huge shell middens that at times reach a depth of 3.5 metres. Fish bones are common in South Cave, a pointer to its early occupation as no such bones have been found so far in sites dating from about 3,800 years ago.

Middens of packed shells and bones, especially those of elephant seals, are a feature at West Point, towards the north of the west coast. Deposits of this type provide valuable information about the lifestyle and prey of the Aborigines. They demonstrate, for instance, that elephant seals, whose breeding range is now confined to Macquarie Island, must have had a colony near West Point as the remains include those of young calves.

Early French explorers noted Aboriginal artwork, as did George Augustus Robinson, remembered as the "conciliator" responsible for the rounding up of the last tribal Aborigines, who reported seeing artwork on the walls of Aboriginal huts and burial structures on the west coast. Rock art at Mount Cameron West, known to Aborigines as Preminghana, was not found until 1933, despite the fact that Robinson passed near the site with a band of Aborigines during the 1830s. It is presumed that the work must have been covered with thickly vegetated sand at that time, but subsequent wind erosion along the coastal dunes has exposed the motifs of geometric designs and the tracks of animals and birds.

This art, which is an integral part of Tasmanian Aboriginal culture, is similar to some found on mainland Australia, especially in the central desert. It shows that the traditional art forms brought by Aborigines travelling to Tasmania before the island was cut off by Bass Strait were also practised by their

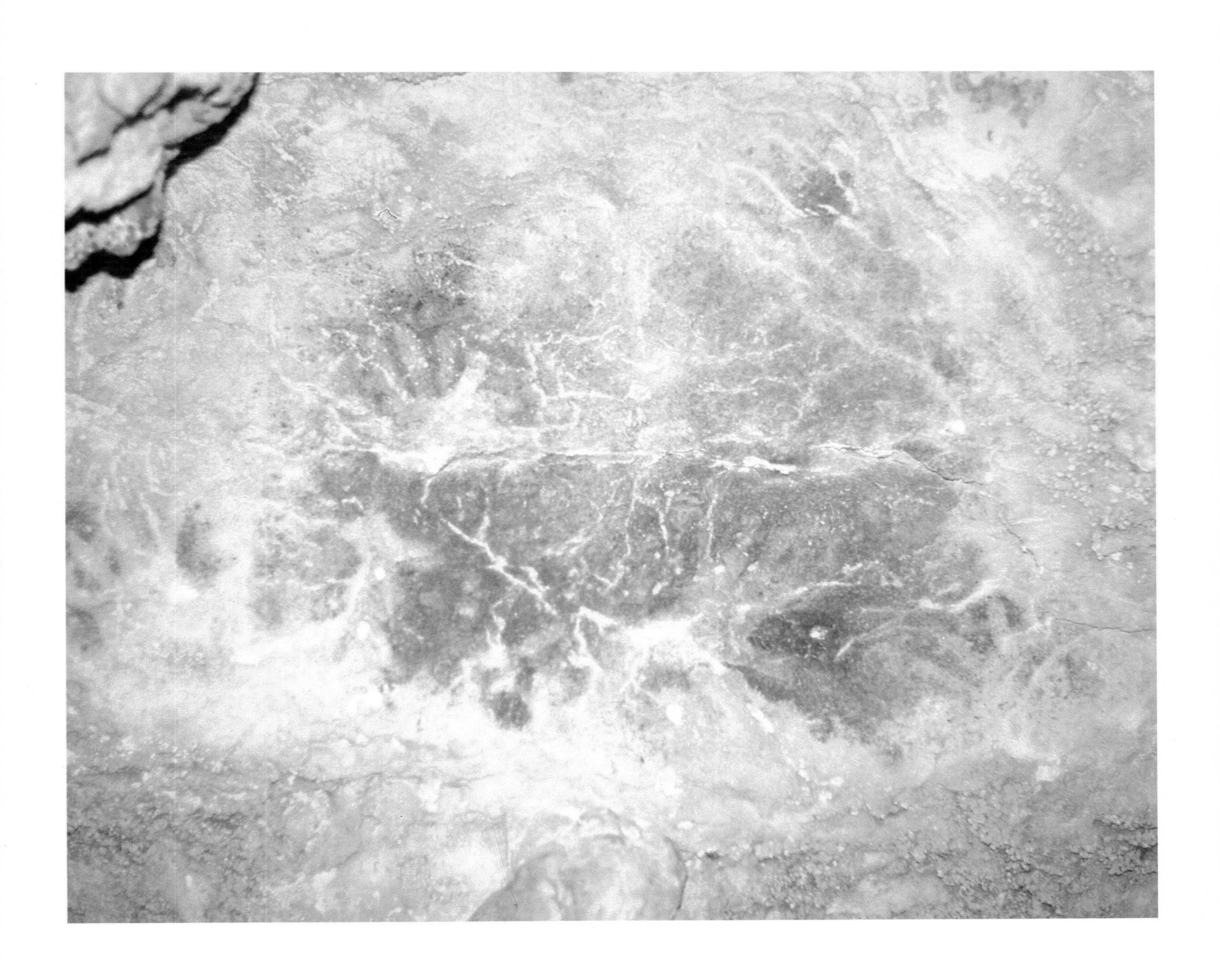

◀
The highest concentration of Tasmanian Aborigines was formerly found in the area that became the 'Woolnorth' property on the island's north-western tip

▶
Buttongrass in the South-West was frequently fired by Aboriginies

▼
Aboriginal dinner party (Tasmaniana Library collection)

descendants.

These sites are all under the protection of the Tasmanian Department of Parks, Wildlife and Heritage, which is also responsible for the management of the Aboriginal sites in the World Heritage Area.

The Aborigines used fire extensively to make it easier for them to move across the country, to assist in hunting and for signalling. This burning led to the establishment of the vegetation patterns that confronted the early European explorers, fire-adaptive eucalypts tending to replace the casuarinas and she-oaks that covered wide areas about 40,000 years ago. In Tasmania, the dense forest was the main barrier to penetration by Europeans and the first settlements were made in open country that had been established by the Aborigines.

Ironically, after thousands of years as hunters of Tasmania's land and sea, the Aboriginal race that observed the first white men on these shores was wiped out within 234 years of the visit by Dutch navigator Abel Janszoon Tasman, who is credited with the modern-day discovery of Tasmania in 1642.

Lieutenant-Governor Collins had declared in 1810 that "any person offering violence to a native or in cool blood murdering one, should be dealt with by laws as if such violence or murder had been committed on a civilized person." However, by 1830, following mounting retaliation by the natives, Governor Arthur decided that military and civilian forces should round up the Aborigines and contain them in a restricted area, the Tasman Peninsula. Despite the promise of rewards of £5 for each adult

▶
Recreated settler's hut, Risdon Cove

▼
Wybalenna Chapel (Photo: Tourism Tasmania)

and £2 for each child captured alive, this Black Line operation, which cost the government £35,000 (more than half its annual budget), failed miserably. Only two native people were rounded up.

The next efforts concentrated on conciliation, with bricklayer George Augustus Robinson being given the task of travelling the island to meet with natives and persuade them to be taken to a place where he said they would be cared for but would no longer have to contend with the people who had become their aggressors. Sadly this was not to be the case.

By the end of 1830, 56 natives had been captured and placed on Swan Island in Bass Strait. They were later moved to Vansittart Island and then to Flinders Island. In 5 years, nearly 200 Aborigines were captured, but about two-thirds of them died between 1835 and 1842, and only a small number of children were born in the same period. Wybalenna (Aboriginal for blackmen's houses), which was their base, effectively became a concentration camp.

Only 45 Aborigines were left after 15 years and, in 1847, they were moved to Oyster Cove, south of Hobart. The last members of the group were William Lanney (King Billy), who died in March 1869, and Truganini, the daughter of a chief of the Bruni tribe, who lived until May 1876.

At Wybalenna, a brick chapel, now restored by the National Trust, and the commandant's quarters are the only buildings in existence that were associated with the Aborigines. The Wybalenna area is the subject of a land claim by the present Tasmanian Aboriginal community, which wants to protect the spirits of the Aborigines who died there and to return the remains that were removed from graves - usually for scientific studies.

Referring to the demise of the former Oyster Bay, Big River, Stony Creek and Western tribes, author John West wrote in "The History of Tasmania", published in 1852, that *"No man can witness the triumph of colonisation, when cities rise in the desert, and the wilderness blossoms as the rose, without being gladdened by the change; but the question which includes the fate of the aborigines - What will become of them? - must check exultation.... At length the secret comes out: the tribe which welcomed the first settler with shouts and dancing, or at worst looked on with indifference, has ceased to live."*

The current Tasmanian population includes about 6,700 descendants of the Aborigines. At one time, Aboriginality was considered to be a quality that should be hidden because of fear of discrimination and prejudice, but today's Aboriginal community, descendants of the original Tasmanians, proudly assert their identity. There is a great resurgence of interest and appreciation of Aboriginal heritage to be found in rock art, stone arrangements and sacred sites around the island.

Although the initial European settlement was primarily by the British, Tasmania is now a stronghold for settlers from many countries. The Chinese, in particular, have contributed to the heritage of this State. Hundreds of them headed to Tasmania during the gold boom at Garibaldi, in the North-East, and the subsequent tin mining boom of the 19th century.

Industrial development after World War 11, especially that involving the generation of hydro-electricity, attracted migrants from around the globe, notably Italians, Greeks, Dutch, Finns, Poles and other eastern Europeans. They have all played a part in the development of the present-day multi-cultural society.

The explorers of the 17th and 18th centuries were from a number of nations, too. Dutch, French and British seamen were driven along the Roaring Forties, trade winds that blow from west to east in the band between the 40th and 50th parallels of latitude. As Tasmania is on the edge of this wind belt it was often the initial landfall for those sailing the oceans in search of new lands, trading posts and treasures.

The first of these explorers to set foot on Tasmanian soil was a Dutch sea captain, Abel Tasman, who landed on the Forestier Peninsula and near Blackman Bay on the east coast. Earlier, he had named the island "Anthony Van Diemenslandt", in honour of the Governor of Batavia, after sighting the

mountainous west coast on 24 November 1642. The shortened version, Van Diemen's Land, was changed to Tasmania in 1856.

Tasman was in charge of the vessels *Heemskerk* and *Zeehan*, which had been despatched from the Batavian capital, Java, by the Dutch East India Company. The aims of the voyage were to learn more about land thought to exist between New Guinea and Australia's west coast and to find a southern route from Java to Chile. Instead, Tasman found Tasmania and New Zealand, before returning to Java on a route north of New Guinea.

It was another 130 years before Tasmania was visited again, French navigator Marc-Joseph Marion du Fresne also anchoring on the east coast. Marion Bay, named after him, is one of many places - especially in the East and South-East - that bear names bestowed by Dutch, English and French explorers.

The visit by du Fresne was the first in which contact was made with the Tasmanian Aborigines. It was an ominous encounter, with one of the natives being killed by gunfire.

The next to come were the British - Captain Tobias Furneaux (1773), Captain James Cook (1777), who landed at Adventure Bay, Bruny Island, and tied his vessel to a tree that still exists and is known as Cook's Tree, Captain William Bligh (1788) and Captain John Henry Cox (1789), who charted parts of the south coast, including the bay named Cox Bight, and explored the strait between Maria Island and the east coast.

In 1792, a navigational error resulted in French Admiral A.R.J. Bruny D'Entrecasteaux discovering the channel between Bruny Island and the Tasmanian mainland, and becoming the first European to sail up the River Derwent (then called Riviere du Nord).

He was followed in 1794 by Commodore John Hayes, who charted sections of the river, which he re-named Derwent. Hayes was the first to sight New Norfolk and named Risdon Cove, where a settlement was established in 1803.

The coastline of Tasmania, especially around King and Flinders Islands, is dotted with shipwrecks, the sinking of the *Sydney Cove* in Bass Strait in 1797 ultimately leading to the discovery of the waters that were to become known as Bass Strait.

The vessel went down between Clarke Island and Cape Barren Island and, months later, a rescue party despatched from Port Jackson found survivors and cargo on nearby Preservation Island.

A reserve protects the remains of the *Sydney Cove*, which has been the subject of intensive archaeological and conservation work by the Queen Victoria Museum, Launceston, and the Launceston Maritime Museum. Artefacts recovered from the vessel form part of a major *Sydney Cove* display in the Maritime Museum, which is based in an 1842 merchant's warehouse and residence that is also on the Register of the National Estate.

Formal possession of Tasmania was taken by Governor Arthur Phillip on 26 January 1788, but it was still not known whether this was, in fact, an island. The point was proved in 1798 during a whaleboat voyage by Lieutenant Matthew Flinders and Surgeon George Bass, who circumnavigated the island, beginning on a westerly course along the north coast. They were accompanied as far as Cape Barren Island by Captain Charles Bishop, who set up a sealing camp at Kent Bay. Although it is not generally credited as such, this was the first British settlement in Tasmania.

Further exploration of the south-east coast by the French when Admiral Nicholas Baudin arrived in 1802 led to a decision by Governor King, of New South Wales, that permanent settlements were needed if British sovereignty of Tasmania was to be retained.

This resulted in the establishment of a settlement at Risdon Cove in 1803 and subsequent ones at Sullivans Cove and Port Dalrymple, in the North, in 1804.

Risdon Cove is the only settlement site of an Australian capital city to retain any semblance of its original form. Now managed by the Tasmanian Department of Parks, Wildlife and Heritage, marked areas show the position of huts and there is a flagpole where the original flagstaff stood. Roll call was held at this spot each day, with officers reading the latest colonial instructions. Other historic evidence is housed in a pyramid-shaped interpretation centre.

The first store, the ruins of which are the oldest colonial stone structure, is near the point where Lieutenant John Bowen and his party landed after sailing up the River Derwent in the *Albion* and the *Lady Nelson* on 11 September 1803. The group consisted of 49 free, convict and military personnel.

A replica of the brigantine *Lady Nelson* has become a familiar sight on the Derwent since her commissioning in 1989. The 53-foot vessel is owned by the Tasmanian Sail Training Association and members of the public interested in the recreation of this link with the island's heritage contributed to the cost of construction. One of the most important roles of the *Lady Nelson* is as a sail training vessel, enabling Tasmanians of the present to turn back the clock to the days when sail reigned supreme on these waters.

The Risdon Cove camp, which was the site of the first major massacre of Aborigines (a hunting party of 300 men, women and children who were driving kangaroos into the cove), proved to be short-lived. Inadequate water supplies and the lack of a good landing place led to its closure soon after Lieutenant Bowen and most of his people returned to Port Jackson on 9 August 1804. The decision to close it down was made by Lieutenant-Governor David Collins, who had established a new settlement at Hobart, on the shores of the Derwent harbour, one of the world's finest deepwater harbours. Even today, much of Hobart's life revolves around the waterfront and the River Derwent, the praises of which were eloquently sung by newspaper editor Henry Melville, writing in the "Van Diemen's Land Annual of 1834"...

"The Derwent River is most notable and magnificent, varying in width from its entrance to Hobart Town, from six to twelve miles, having everywhere deep water, without rocks or sand bars, and navigable in all seasons, even by a stranger, with the most perfect ease and safety."

From an initial settlement of 300 people, Hobart Town soon expanded beyond the main Macquarie Street precinct, which is noted today for its fine sandstone buildings that are considered to be among the best of Australia's colonial architecture. By 1805, buildings were appearing in the first suburb, New Town, and considerable development was also taking place in the North along the Tamar River.

Exploration of the Tamar Valley began in 1798 following the discovery of the Tamar estuary by Bass and Flinders during their circumnavigation of Tasmania. They named Port Dalrymple at the river mouth. In 1804, Lieutenant-Governor Collins, who was based at Port Phillip Bay, Victoria, before setting out for the Derwent, decided to send William Collins to explore the Tamar and report on its suitability for settlement. The voyage, once again in the *Lady Nelson*, took him as far as the Cataract Gorge, where the South Esk River falls into the Tamar through a chasm between very steep, rocky banks. However, by the time the expeditioners returned to Port Phillip

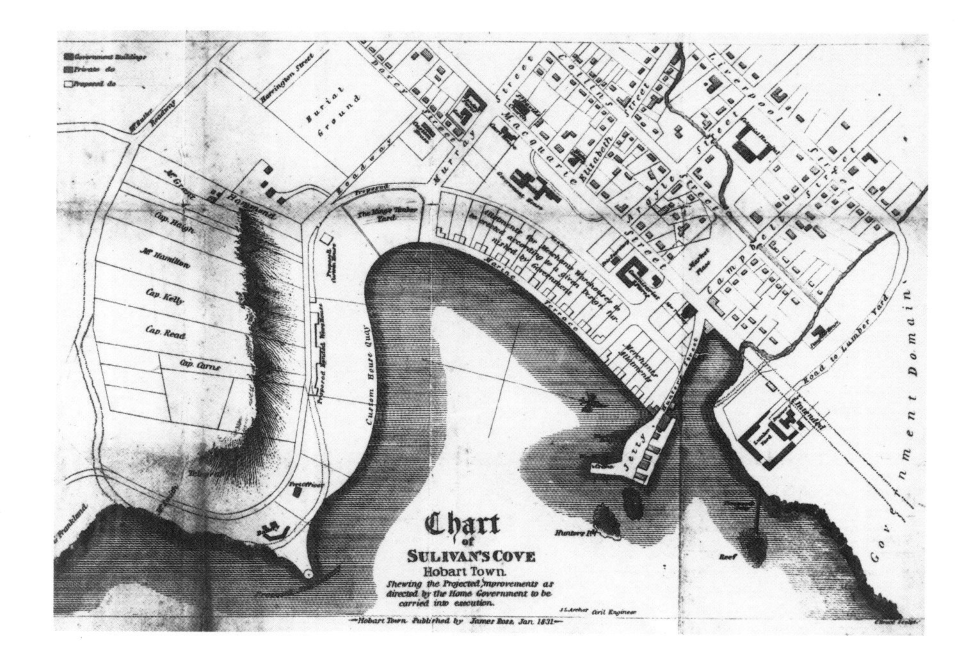

▶
An early residence on Hobart's outskirts - Pitt's Farm, Moonah - built in the 1820s as a country retreat of Richard Pitt, the chief constable of southern Tasmania (Photo by permission of Mr Ernie Phythian)

◀
Early chart of Sullivans Cove (Tasmaniana Library collection)

Bay, Lieutenant-Governor Collins had decided on the Derwent settlement site and was already preparing to depart.

Soon afterwards, Governor King received a despatch from Lord Hobart, the Secretary of State for the Colonies, recommending the settlement of Port Dalrymple and nominating Lieutenant-Colonel William Paterson, of the New South Wales Corps, as Lieutenant-Governor of the new colony. This ultimately resulted in Paterson making two attempts to reach the Tamar, the second time proving successful. The *Lady Nelson* continued her sterling role, along with other expedition vessels - the *Francis*, *Integrity* and *Buffalo*, the latter of which contributed to the decision on a landing site after running aground and being brought to anchor in Outer Cove, now George Town. Colonel Paterson landed at the cove with a party of 181 people on 11 November 1804 and hoisted the Union Jack.

After re-establishing his headquarters a short time later at York Town, on the western side of the Tamar mouth, Paterson eventually conceded that this was not a suitable site. Hence, as in the early days of southern settlement, the main base was moved to the present-day city site. Launceston, which was originally called Patersonia, had its beginnings in March 1806.

Confusion on the status of Collins and Paterson, who had both been named Lieutenant-Governor, was resolved by Governor King, who divided Tasmania at the 42° parallel and made each man sovereign in his own half, but subordinate to him. This left Paterson in charge of the County of Cornwall and Collins heading the County of Buckingham. Although this dividing line no longer officially exists, people in the northern and southern sectors of the State still display parochial differences as they vie for superiority.

Many of the early villages, such as Ross and Oatlands, were military barracks. This was very much a land of the military, free settlers, convicts who had been transported from Britain to the penal establishments of Van Diemen's Land and the original inhabitants - the Aborigines.

The subject of land grants or, more correctly, land rights for white settlers, is still regarded as discriminatory by the Tasmanian Aboriginal community in relation to black land rights.

The island's population received a significant boost when settlers began arriving from the Norfolk Island penal settlement in 1807, notably in the New Norfolk and Longford districts. Each free settler received four acres of land for every one acre held on Norfolk Island and they were guaranteed rations until they became self-sufficient. This was quite a bonus considering food was in short supply during the early days of the colony.

Later, a Land Grants Scheme was introduced to ensure that no Tasmanian settlers could receive a greater extent of land than they were capable of improving and that grants could not be made to people who planned to dispose of them. By 1831, land sales had replaced the system of free land grants.

In encouraging free settlers to migrate, "The Hobart Town Monthly Magazine" of 1833 listed the ideal attributes as *"industry, perseverance, sobriety and patience, with a tolerable share of judgment and caution - in one word, unvarying steadiness. If we are to add a small capital of a few hundred pounds, the freaks of Fortune must be very capricious indeed if their possessor does not succeed in his heart's content."*

By this stage, both the free settlers and many of the convicts had contributed much to the modern-day settlement and development of Tasmania, although total assimilation was still a long way off when this report appeared in 1831 in "A Statistical View of Van Diemen's Land":

"There is probably a larger proportion of intelligent well informed persons in Hobart-town than in most communities of the same size in any other part of the world. This arises in part from its being the seat of Government, and from the number of respectable persons whom it necessarily employs and draws round it, from its being the capital of the island, and the grand focus, as it were, of consumption on the one side, and of supply on the other with all parts of the interior, thereby affording profitable employment for a considerable body of commercial men and people in business, - and from the circumstance that few but men of intelligence and ability, of strong minds, and bold, spirited enterprise would venture in the first instance to undertake the long and arduous voyage to so remote a country, and to struggle with the numerous and unavoidable difficulties, the hardships and privations incidental to a new colony.

We have besides frequently heard it remarked that part of this advanced character of society in Hobart-town is to be attributed to the convict population, of which many individuals are unquestionably possessed of superior skills in their several occupations and of very considerable talents, and that the very fact of their having brought these into their present condition is a proof that they are possessed of peculiar qualifications, or at least of eccentric properties of disposition bursting as they have done from the everyday circle of ordinary life, in order to arrive at pleasure or profit by a shorter course and more summary method than the rest of mankind.

But we will never allow that either the wealth or property, much less the respectability of a community, can be increased by such men."

Time has mellowed these views...

▶
The Lady Nelson - present and past

Exploration

The original Hobart-Launceston road was surveyed in 1812, but overland exploration was well under way five years earlier when Lieutenant Thomas Laycock travelled on horseback from Port Dalrymple to Hobart on an inland route that passed through what is now Bothwell.

The first section of the highway, generally referred to in times gone by as the Main Road, was laid between Hobart Town and Austins Ferry in 1819. Work also began at the northern end, with convicts involved in the roadwork being stationed at various points along the route.

Other early road-building included the route from Launceston to Longford. In 1813 the roadmaker rendered an account for £13, but agreed instead to accept "one cow in lieu thereof"! At this stage the Longford district was home to many settlers from Norfolk Island. After the road was finished there was a further influx of settlers, including a number of people who had held posts in the Imperial Service in New South Wales and Tasmania.

Homes of distinction were built, some of which are still owned by descendants of the pioneers - a feature of the Tasmanian rural community that is not found to such a large extent in other parts of Australia.

As explorers and settlers pushed out from the two main centres they often encountered difficulties with the terrain, fast-flowing streams posing a particular hazard. Other problems arose as settlers took up land for farming that Aborigines had used previously for their own hunting and other food-gathering.

The Europeans and Aborigines had totally different ideas about property and property rights. The Aborigines did not understand the motives of settlers who regarded them as intruders if they entered the newly established boundaries. The inevitable conflict was further exasperated by bushrangers (usually escaped convicts) who plundered farms and committed additional atrocities against the Aborigines.

Many of Tasmania's older country houses incorporate design features that were aimed at protecting the inhabitants against attack. In addition to lookout towers, heavy bolts and locks, there are less-obvious inclusions. Some properties, for

▲
Mt Roland - one of many mountains that posed hazards to colonial explorers

◀
The Central Plateau was first traversed by white men in the 1820s

HENRY HELLYER ESQUIRE
obiit
2 september 1832
A 42

▲
Hollow trees provided refuge for travellers

◀▲▲
"Highfield", once the headquarters of the Van Diemen's Land Company

◀▲
Outbuildings at "Highfield"

◀
The grave of surveyor Henry Hellyer in the Stanley cemetery

instance, have underground rooms that could be barricaded and, in the case of places like "Cluny" at Bothwell, there is even a peephole below ground level that enabled the residents to view activities on the approach to the house.

Bothwell, situated on the Clyde River (formerly called Fat Doe River), was first settled permanently by Charles Rowcroft, who left Hobart in 1817. Scottish emigrants flocked to the township in the 1820s and it soon developed as an important agricultural area as well as being the district headquarters for the military. Today, Bothwell is living history, the sandstone cottages, old stores, churches and country mansions presenting a similar image to that of 150 years ago.

The 1820s was a key period for inland exploration, mainly because the Van Diemen's Land Company decided to operate in the island, there was a need for more pastoral land and a considerable amount of encouragement was offered by an official surveyor, George Frankland, who went on to become Surveyor-General.

The Van Diemen's Land Company, which was established in 1825, is the last of the Royal Charter companies that were set up to reap the wealth of Britain's colonies. Its prized holding is "Woolnorth", a 23,000-hectare sheep and cattle property on the north-west tip of Tasmania.

The original order of the company was to select land "beyond the ramparts of the unknown." This area, which had the island's highest concentration of Aboriginal inhabitants, was chosen after extensive exploration in a westerly direction along the northern coast. En route, the newcomers made use of some very basic accommodation... They were amazed at the remarkably large stringybark trees that had been hollowed out by fires lit by natives, an example of Aboriginal technology involving the use of natural resources to achieve the same end as those of European house construction. Some members of the party sought shelter in these trees, with bark forming a porch and door. Recounting his travels of Van Diemen's Land, in his 1829 Almanack, printer James Ross said *"a room both comodious and comfortable was formed sufficient for the parlour and bedroom of six or eight men, who lived in it for some time."*

The most notable surveyor involved in early north-western exploration was Henry Hellyer, whose gravestone is in the Stanley cemetery.

The Van Diemen's Land Company developed headquarters at the "Highfield Estate" at Circular Head, a property that is now owned by the Tasmanian Government. Nearby, the ruins of barracks that once housed convicts serve as a reminder of the valuable role played by these men in opening up Tasmania's hinterland.

While the company was establishing its grazing interests at "Woolnorth" it was also contributing to the advancement of Stanley, one of the State's finest historic townships.

An unfulfilled aim of company officials was to create a route through the centre of the island

▲
Timber was a drawcard in the D'Entrecasteaux Channel area

▶
A bullock-driver's lament preserved for posterity on the east coast!

from the far north-western section to Hobart. Among those who traversed the central region during the 1820s was Danish-born adventurer Jorgen Jorgenson, one of the more colourful Tasmanian explorers. During the Napoleonic Wars he had installed himself as the King of Iceland, but he later returned to England and was subsequently transported for pawning the linen from his lodgings. Jorgenson was recommended as a bushman capable of leading an expedition to search for a route between the Derwent and Circular Head settlements.

Today, the central part of Tasmania, especially the Cradle Mountain-Lake St Clair National Park, is trekked by thousands of people each year. They often follow in the footsteps of a 20th century explorer and naturalist, Gustav Weindorfer, who bought land in the Cradle Valley in 1911 and built a forest home he called "Waldheim". Weindorfer, a father of the Tasmanian conservation movement, was a prime force in having Cradle Mountain declared a reserve in 1922. A replica of Weindorfer's guest house was re-built in 1978 by the National Parks and Wildlife Service from hand-hewn King Billy pine. Situated at the northern end of the national park, on the site of the original building, it highlights an aspect of Tasmanian heritage that is now appreciated by visitors who come from all over the globe to experience the sheer beauty of this still partially untamed area.

White explorers began to venture into the Huon region in the 1820s but initial reports claimed that the area was too thickly timbered for settlement. Later, it was this timber of the Huon, D'Entrecasteaux Channel and Geeveston areas that drew people to the district, although some settlement had already taken place near Southport, where there was a whaling station. Coastal shipping services were established to transport the products of mills and other forestry operations long before roads linked the major centres. By contrast, travellers were using a road to the more-open east coast as early as the 1830s. Sections of the Tasman Highway still follow the same route.

The North-East was not extensively explored until the 1840s, the propensity of mountains having discouraged pastoralists. The first expeditions were led by government surveyor James Scott, after whom Scottsdale was named. He was so impressed with the land near Ringarooma that he selected acreage and called the property "Legerwood".

Even today, access to the South-West, with its rugged terrain and, at times, dense vegetation, is often difficult. In the early part of the 19th century most travellers arrived by sea. Port Davey was one of the ports of call for Captain James Kelly, who circumnavigated Tasmania in 1815/16. The voyage took 49 days, the small, five-oared whaleboat *Elizabeth* never being out of the sight of land. An overland expedition to the South-West was undertaken in the 1830s by George Augustus Robinson, who was led to Port Davey by Aborigines

▲ *"Waldheim" - a recreation of the forest home established by naturalist Gustav Weindorfer in the Cradle Valley*

Wooredy and Truganini. He then journeyed to the Arthur Range before travelling north to Macquarie Harbour.

The early white explorers frequently followed "roads" established by Aboriginal people for the purpose of trade, ceremony and seasonal migration. These routes ran along the coast and into the highlands.

The western region was the last to be tackled by colonial explorers. This was partly because officials wanted to keep the Macquarie Harbour penal establishments isolated. The position reversed when many Tasmanians left to seek their fortunes during the Victorian gold rush of the 1850s, and the Tasmanian Government was urged to initiate a gold search closer to home. Several expeditions were led by an English geologist, Charles Gould, who eventually found traces of copper, lead and gold along the Gordon and Franklin Rivers in 1862. Gould had spent time close to the deposits that later formed the basis of the Mount Lyell Company's century-plus mining operations at Queenstown, but his reports concluded that there was insufficient gold for a viable mining venture. Eventually it was copper, not gold, that helped to fill Mount Lyell's coffers, while modern-day explorers have continued the search for more wealth from this highly mineralised region.

It wasn't until the 1930s that Queenstown, the main west coast centre, was connected to Hobart by road, the completion of the Lyell Highway and, more recently, the Murchison Highway between Zeehan, in the West, and Burnie, via Hampshire, on the north-west coast, forming the culmination of what is essentially 30,000 years of exploration, surveying and roadbuilding that has linked Tasmania and opened it up for settlement.

The Sea

▲
Strahan - a long-time haven for seafarers

◀
Signal station in Princes Park, Battery Point

With no part of Tasmania more than 115 kilometres from the sea life revolves to a large extent around the coastal waters for industry and leisure. This has been so for thousands of years and nowadays the greatest proportion of the island's 451,000 inhabitants lives in coastal areas.

The early 19th century settlements depended entirely upon the sea for their communications, with vessels of many kinds bringing supplies that were unobtainable in the colony.

The first news of imminent arrivals in the South was usually sent via a signal station at the top of Mount Nelson and a relay station at Battery Point. The latter was established in 1818 as a guard house for soldiers of the Mulgrave Battery and is now the oldest building in Battery Point. Messages could also be relayed from a signal station at Port Arthur, with information about convict escapes being received in Hobart within a few minutes.

Tasmania is well endowed with waters that harbour an abundance of seafoods such as molluscs (abalone, scallops, oysters and mussels), crustaceans (southern rock lobster, generally called crayfish) and fin fish, including jack mackerel, flounder, barracouta, shark, orange roughy, trevalla and tuna. The exploitation of many of these resources has led to the development of industries that form part of Tasmania's heritage. Likewise with whaling, which was the backbone of the early 19th century colony, and sealing - now both pursuits of the past.

◀
"Secheron House" - base for Maritime Museum of Tasmania

◀
Museum display

Herds of seals were discovered by Europeans in Bass Strait in the 18th century, but within a decade of the first sealing camp being established on the south coast of Cape Barren Island in 1798 the seals had been hunted almost to extinction. The sealers were tough and ruthless, with a number of them remaining on Bass Strait islands after the demise of the sealing. Aboriginal women, many of whom were kidnapped by the sealers, became their companions, leading to the founding of Aboriginal communities on many of the islands of the Furneaux Group, notably Cape Barren Island.

The muttonbird industry - one of the oldest in Australia - was started by the sealers and Aboriginal women in the 1820s, although Aborigines had gathered and traded the birds long before this time.

During the 19th century, muttonbirds were caught for their oil, which was used for medicinal purposes and, most importantly, for their feathers, which were exported to German pillow and bedding manufacturers. Nowadays, canned muttonbirds (shearwaters) are regarded as a gourmet line, but it is not the first time they have been presented in this form. In World War 11 muttonbirds canned on Flinders island were sold to American troops as squab in aspic!

Whaling was Tasmania's most important maritime industry in the 1800s, Tasmanian whaleboats being among the most perfectly modelled boats of modern times. Part of this past has been preserved in the form of a 28-foot Huon pine replica of the whaleboat *Elizabeth*, which was lent to Captain James Kelly for his early voyage around Tasmania. Launched in 1985, the new Hobart-based whaleboat is used at regattas, historical re-enactments and for educational purposes associated with the State's history.

Scrimshaw, the art of working ivory, whalebone or shell, became a hobby for crew members during whaling voyages, the bones and teeth of sperm whales being turned into decorative and utilitarian objects. Collections of these intricate creations are displayed in a number of centres, including the Tasmanian Museum and Art Gallery, the Tasmaniana Collection at the State Library and the Maritime Museum of Tasmania, all in Hobart, the Queen Victoria Museum and Art Gallery, Launceston, the maritime museum at Low Head and the Launceston Maritime Museum. The Tasmanian Museum and Art Gallery also has harpoons, boat lines, ambergris, which came from the intestines of sperm whales and was used as a perfume fixative, a model of the whaling barque *Lady Emma*, built in Battery Point and launched in 1848, and other artefacts and records related to the whaling industry. Whales were pursued by British, French and American whalers well before Lieutenant Bowen established his settlement at Risdon Cove in 1803. At that stage, Waub's Boat Harbour (now known as Bicheno) was used by sealers and whalers seeking shelter for their boats. The name "Waub" is believed to have come from an Aboriginal woman, Waubedebar, whose fenced grave at Bicheno has a tombstone "erected in her memory by a few of her white friends." Waubedebar had been a victim of "gin catching" by whalers and sealers but she earned their respect after rescuing two men, including her de-facto husband, from near-drowning. She was also particularly generous to pioneers of the east coast.

The first whaling station in the colony was established in 1806 at Tryworks Point, near Ralphs Bay, by William Collins, a relative of Lieutenant-Governor Collins. Before long, bay whaling, which involved hunting in land-based whaleboats rather than in craft from a mother ship, was undertaken from at least 40 stations around the coastline.

Hobart's initial development was funded to a large extent by the whaling industry. An issue of the Hobart Town Gazette stated that *"whaling was without doubt the grand prop and stay of the colonies. In those days bay whaling was in full swing, and the most important asset to the Colony. By 1816 tryworks stations were scattered all along the shores of Bruny Island, south to Recherche Bay, at Bicheno and Wineglass Bay on the East Coast. At each station greasy black barrels were ranged along the clean white beaches and skeletons of whales flanked the boatsheds and slipways. The lookouts commanded a wide stretch of ocean and at their signals the boats would be manned, sometimes a dozen rival boats setting out after the same whale. Capturing an infuriated fighting monster was no picnic, and often boats were smashed and men drowned; but the price of the oil made the game worth the candle, and there was no lack of stout lads offering."*

By 1835 Hobart had become the greatest whaling port in the British seas and a base for English, French and American whalers ranging right across the southern hemisphere. However, bay and offshore whaling declined by the 1880s and the last local whaling voyage, in the barque *Helen*, took place in 1899.

Other fisheries with a long history include abalone-gathering. Aboriginal women were the first abalone divers in Tasmania, their skills being utilised by early white settlers. The commercial abalone fishery dates from 1964 and it has become so lucrative that licences are required for divers supplying the export market.

Crayfish, scallop, squid and other sea fisheries have also contributed substantially to Tasmania's income over the years and have helped to sustain fishing ports like Kettering, Dover, Triabunna, Strahan, Stanley, Bridport, St Helens, Bicheno, Dunalley, Currie on King Island and Lady Barron on Flinders Island.

Shipbuilding remains an important maritime industry. During the 19th century a number of prospering merchants also became shipowners. Local boatbuilders, notably those at Battery Point, in the D'Entrecasteaux Channel area, the Huon and the Tamar regions, did good business - especially in the construction of clippers made

▲
Tasman Island lighthouse

▶▲
Lighthouse at Low Head

▶▶
Museum in Low Head Pilot station

▶▼
Cottages in Pilot Station complex

from local bluegum. Tasmania's famed Huon pine was also a prime timber for ships because of its durability, but with supplies now limited the heyday of Huon pine shipbuilding is well and truly over.

Bluegum and New Zealand kauri pine were used in the paddle steamer *Kangaroo*, which became the first twin-hulled craft in service on the Derwent when she went on the run in 1855. Catamarans are still being built in Hobart, but now it is mighty wave-piercing aluminium craft of well over 70 metres that are sought by overseas as well as local shipping companies. The builders, International Catamarans Proprietary Limited, earned themselves a place in history books when one of their catamarans won the Hales Trophy for the fastest crossing of the Atlantic by a passenger vessel, during a delivery voyage to the United Kingdom in 1990.

Another name in the chronicles of Tasmanian shipping is Holyman. In the second half of the 19th century Captain William Holyman, of Launceston, established a fleet of small sailing vessels and steamers that traded between King Island, Launceston and Melbourne. The Holyman family was also involved in early aviation and the name lives on in the extensive shipping services of William Holyman and Sons.

Generations of the O'May family have also contributed to Tasmanian seafaring, especially the 20th century Derwent ferry services.

The colourful history of Hobart's ferries dates back to 1816, when Urics Allander took goods and passengers across the harbour and James Austin established an important link for travel between Hobart and Launceston by running a ferry service across the river at what is now called Austins Ferry, in the city of Glenorchy. This was well before the days of the Bridgewater causeway.

The 194-tonne *Cartela* is the sole survivor of fleets of wooden ferries that used to be a familiar sight on the Derwent. Built in 1912 by Purdon and Featherstone for the Huon, Channel and Peninsula Steamship Company, the *Cartela* was referred to as the "river greyhound", her services being increased during World War 1 to include patrol duties.

In bygone times, ferry races were an integral part of many regattas - aquatic carnivals that are just as popular today as when the first ones were held in Tasmania more than 140 years ago. The Royal Hobart Regatta, the biggest aquatic event in the southern hemisphere, started in 1838. The foreshore at Pavilion Point was lined with 5,000 people waiting to see the Governor, Sir John Franklin, and Lady Franklin, arrive in the government barge. A highlight of proceedings on that day was a whaleboat race in which 15 craft competed over a six-mile course.

The Sandy Bay Regatta, first held in 1849 where Wrest Point Casino now stands, New Norfolk Regatta and Bellerive Regatta are among others that have stood the test of time.

Some of Tasmania's veteran vessels are now interstate visitor attractions but the island still retains a core of craft that have contributed to its maritime history.

The *Defender*, a 67-tonne ketch built in New South Wales of red gum and launched in 1896, was restored recently by her Launceston owner, who had the derelict hull towed from Hobart to the Tamar for repairs and re-fitting. The *Defender* made history in 1923 when she crossed from Smithton to Port Phillip Heads, Victoria, in 18.5 hours - a record time at that stage.

The *May Queen*, which is berthed permanently at Watermans Dock, Hobart, is a 36-tonne ketch that belonged to the Chesterman family for well over 50 years. Launched in 1867, she was one of the first classy fast ketches on the Derwent and carried timber from mills in the Huon, North and North-East and on the east coast.

The Enterprise, named after the schooner in which John Pascoe Fawkner and John Batman sailed from Tasmania to found the city of Melbourne, was also on the timber run - as well as having a role in the 1926 production of the film "For the Term of his Natural Life", shot at Port Arthur. The 1902 ketch is is now based on land at Bicheno.

The small Huon pine cutter *Matilda* is a feature at Port Arthur. Launched in 1896, the *Matilda* was a fishing boat before starting a 40-year service carrying mail to the tiny community of lighthouse keepers and their families on Tasman Island, off the south-east coast.

The lighthouses around Tasmania have played a vital role in exploration and development of the island, providing navigational aid, communication links and weather monitoring services. The first light was erected in 1832 on the Iron Pot islet at the mouth of the River Derwent and at one stage there was even a lighthouse keeper's residence on the small, rocky outcrop. The convict-built Cape Bruny lighthouse, which started working in 1838, is the oldest continually operated lighthouse in Australia. The original Low Head light at the eastern entrance to the Tamar River was also fully operational by 1838, sperm whale oil being used in the lamp, which revolved by clockwork machinery that had to be wound up by hand every eight hours. The present lighthouse dates from 1889.

The Bruny Island lighthouse and the first one at Low Head were designed by civil engineer and colonial architect John Lee Archer, who also designed the earliest buildings of the Low Head Pilot Station. This station, which has been restored by the Port of Launceston Authority and houses a maritime museum, forms part of northern Tasmania's most outstanding group of surviving early colonial buildings.

The only lighthouses that are still manned are at Currie, on King Island, Maatsuyker Island, which is Australia's southermost light, Eddystone Point, on the east coast, and Deal Island, in Bass Strait.

▲▲ *Boat sheds at Cornelian Bay, Hobart*

▲ *"Rossbank Observatory, Hobart", painted by Thomas Bock in 1842 (From the collection of the Tasmanian Museum and Art Gallery)*

▶▲ *Salamanca Place warehouses*

▶▶ *Pots used for crayfishing - one of Tasmania's most lucrative sea fisheries*

The Maatsuyker Island light is a welcome sight for competitors in the annual Melbourne to Hobart Yacht Race as it signals they are near journey's end. The finish of this race coincides with that of the one of the world's most notable yachting events, the Sydney to Hobart Yacht Race, first staged in 1945.

In contrast to today, the earliest Sydney-Hobart race attracted very little attention, nine starters slipping out of Sydney Heads almost unnoticed. *Rani*, the smallest boat in the fleet, won the event outright, a feat not equalled until 1972 when *American Eagle* took out the honours.

The sight of Constitution Dock and adjoining wharves lined with the cream of modern ocean racing yachts is one of Hobart's classic scenes. Add to this the spectacle of rows of sandstone warehouses built in Salamanca Place to service shipping and associated trades, a three-storey bond store dating back to 1815 and former custom houses in Davey Street and the present Parliament House and it is obvious that the influence of the sea extends well beyond the waterline.

The same situation applies in places like Strahan, where a classical custom office was built early this century when this was the main west coast port for the mining industry, in Launceston, with its imposing 1888 Custom House near the Tamar River, and Stanley, whose bluestone bond store built in 1835 from ships' ballast has served a number of purposes over the years. Harbourmasters' houses and slipways, many of which are still functional, continue the story. Turning the clock forward, the dockside activities of busy ports such as Burnie and Devonport demonstrate that the sea is still a vital lifeline for Tasmania.

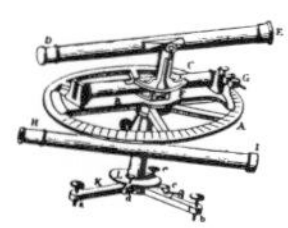

The island's strategic location at the edge of the Indian Ocean and the Tasman Sea, combined with its close proximity to Antarctica, have also made it an important base for scientific research, especially that concerning the sea.

In 1840, Governor Sir John Franklin, who later died in Arctic waters while on an expedition in search of a passage north of Canada, had an observatory built in the grounds of the planned Government House, Hobart. It was established by Captain James Clark Ross when he was in Tasmania en route to the Antarctic in search of the south magnetic pole.

Observations of magnetic variation and other phenomena recorded at the Rossbank Observatory were linked with those of the expeditioners, who spent five months in the Antarctic but were unable to achieve their goal because of the ice barrier. A plaque in Government House grounds marks the site of the observatory, while ruins of part of the complex are evident at the rear entrance of Government House.

Custom Houses in Hobart, Strahan and Launceston

Tasmania has been used regularly as an embarkation point for Antarctic voyages since 1899, when Norwegian-born explorer Carstens Borchgrevinck set off in the *Southern Cross* with a British expedition. One of the most famous farewells was in 1911 when Douglas Mawson sailed on Australia's first major scientific survey of the "Deep South." His destination was Macquarie Island, which was discovered in 1810 and became a Tasmanian dependency in the 1890s. Roald Amundsen, a Norwegian, and his party left Hobart in 1912 and, subsequently, became the first people to reach the South Pole.

Since 1981, Australia's Antarctic headquarters have been based at Kingston, just south of Hobart. This centre coordinates Australia's scientific, political, strategic and economic interests in the Antarctic and sub-Antarctic regions. It is also responsible for the operations of Australia's Antarctic supply vessel, the *Southern Aurora*, which made her maiden voyage in 1990.

The national headquarters for the marine science research of the Commonwealth Scientific and Industrial Research Organisation (CSIRO) are on the Hobart waterfront, in a Marine Laboratories complex that opened in 1985. This is the base for the Divisions of Oceanography and Fisheries, which are involved in national and international projects aimed at increasing knowledge about a broad range of scientific and technological subjects, including the management of fish resources and the role of the sea in climate change.

Australia is responsible for the management of seven million square kilometres of surrounding ocean and Tasmania's research establishments have a vital function in providing information about this marine environment.

▲
Commissariat Bond Store, now part of Tasmanian Museum and Art Gallery

Victoria Dock, Hobart (overleaf)

SEAFARERS RESTAURANT
Ristorante

JAMS

Contribution of Convicts

◀ *Ruins of penitentiary on Sarah Island*

▲ *Convict-built Richmond Bridge has stood the test of time*

Tasmania was a centre for the transportation of convicts from 1803 to 1853, becoming the only such place in the British Empire after 1848. Until 1819 most of the convicts came via Sydney, but after this time there were regular transports direct to the island. The last of Tasmania's colonial penal settlements, at Port Arthur, continued operating for 24 years after the end of transportation. The other major convict settlements were at Macquarie Harbour, on the west coast, and Maria Island, in the East.

About 74,000 convicts were transported to Tasmania, including 14,000 females. Approximately half of them had been sentenced to seven-year terms while one in five were "lifers." However, only those who had committed the more serious crimes were sentenced to a penal establishment, the remainder being assigned to masters as servants or being employed on road gangs or other public works and services.

Convicts were the main source of labour in the first half of the 19th century, with even the police force being largely recruited from their ranks. Following the introduction by the Home Government of a probation system in 1838, about 40 stations were developed around the State to house convicts involved in land-clearing, farming and construction work. These centres included Cascades and Saltwater River on the Tasman Peninsula, Dover, Middleton, Cygnet, Jericho and Colebrook in the South, Fingal to the East and Deloraine, bordering on northern and north-western regions.

Initial convict construction work was controlled by military from the Convict Department but most jobs were designed and directed by the Corps of the Royal Engineers, whose restored Gothic-Revival headquarters in lower Davey Street is now leased by the Institute of Engineers, Australia, from the Tasmanian Government. In 1829, nearly 1,000 of the 1,753 convict labourers were employed in the Engineers' Department.

One of the most arduous jobs was the construction of the Bridgewater causeway between 1830 and 1836. Secondary punishment convicts quarried nearly two million tonnes of sandstone from nearby hills and carted it in barrows to the causeway site. A two-metre high solitary cell that is only 50 centimetres square - the smallest used in Australia - remains near the old watch house on the southern approach to the causeway.

Convicts were a cheap form of labour until 1842, when new regulations were brought in to ensure that a fee was paid for work. By this stage a layered system of prisoner classification was in place. "Ticket of leave" prisoners - those with unexpired sentences who were working as free men, subject to certain conditions - were at the

◀
◀
"Cascades" outstation remains include the former convict hospital (centre) and mess room

◀
King's (later Queen's) School, New Town (Tasmaniana Library collection)

top, followed by assigned servants, those employed in public works and services, road party and chain gang members and, at the lowest level, the inmates of penal settlements.

The harshest penal establishment was on Sarah Island, in Macquarie Harbour, with only the most hardened and undisciplined criminals being sent to this isolated spot during the occupation period between 1822 and 1833. The lash was not spared... records show that nearly all of the 182 prisoners there in the first year received an average of 40 lashes each. In spite of this, they were expected to work hard. They extracted timber from the lower reaches of the Gordon and Franklin Rivers and used the prized Huon pine to build ships. The ruins of a penitentiary on Sarah Island serve as a reminder of this hell-hole on Earth.

By comparison, the convicts sent to Maria Island between 1824 and 1832 had a much easier time. They were "Class 2" prisoners - not considered as incorrigible as those at Sarah Island. Nevertheless, Maria Island was not without its problems and it became notorious for the number of convicts who escaped on rafts or in canoes.

A second convict era, from 1842 to 1850, was somewhat more productive. Prisoners were mainly engaged in agriculture, and a number of substantial buildings erected in this period still survive. They include a mess room, which was also used as a school and a Catholic chapel, a bakehouse and the houses of the Senior Assistant Superintendent and the Assistant Superintendent. The penitentiary, built in 1830 and modified in 1880 and 1920, now provides accommodation for up to 60 visitors - in the space once occupied by 282 convicts!

Port Arthur, the most famous Australian penal settlement, grew out of a need to contain the cost of running small convict depots around the island. The location was ideal because the only means of escape by land was across a narrow isthmus at Eaglehawk Neck, which was constantly guarded. Colonel George Arthur, Lieutenant-Governor of the colony from 1824 to 1836, described it as a "natural penitentiary." A number of outstations were also established on the Tasman Peninsula, Safety Cove being the site of the gaol farm, while up to 400 convicts were engaged in agriculture and timber-cutting at "Cascades", Koonya. The most dreaded work place was the coalmines of Saltwater River, where underground cells provide a chilling insight into the tortuous conditions.

With some convicts as young as only 10 years of age it was necessary to have a special boys' prison so that those up to 18 years old could be separated from the adult convicts. This prison reformatory operated from 1834 to 1848 at Point Puer, five kilometres from the main settlement, and one of the main aims was to train the boys in trades, especially sawying. Ultimately, this also proved beneficial to the fledgling colony.

Education was not overlooked either, convict boys from Point Puer being among those who took lessons at the King's (later Queen's) Orphan School near St John's Church, New Town. They were taken to Hobart by Captain Charles O'Hara Booth, a former commandant at Port Arthur, who was put in charge of the boys in 1848.

The development of skills was not confined to the youth, either. By the 1850s, about 75 different trades were practised at Port Arthur. Products such as flowerpots, tiles, fireplace hobs, clay and bricks were even displayed in international exhibitions in Paris and London. Many Tasmanian buildings contain bricks produced at the Port Arthur brickworks, which operated for 40 years and were one of the first potteries in Tasmania to produce good quality earthenware. Thumb imprints formed when pressure was applied to wet clay being pushed from the brick frames have become a trademark of convict labour, while the broad arrow often found on old bricks traditionally indicated that they were English Government property.

Among those involved in Tasmania's pottery industry was a convict named William Buelow Gould, who worked as a flower painter in a Staffordshire pottery and as an assistant to a London lithographer before being transported to Tasmania. Initially, Gould, whose real surname was Holland, was assigned to attend pottery ovens in Hobart, but his drinking habits landed him in trouble and he was sent to Macquarie Harbour on two occasions. A talented artist, his sketches of Macquarie Harbour are a valuable record of the area in the 1830s. Gould later returned to Hobart, but he was a confirmed drunkard and payment for his paintings of fish, fruit and animals was often in liquid form only!

The Queen Victoria Museum, Launceston, has a comprehensive collection of Gould's work, including three books on Tasmanian flora. His "Book of Fishes", presumably prepared while on the west coast, is in the Allport Library and Museum of Fine Arts, at the State Library, Hobart.

Despite his problems, Gould earned himself a place in Australian art history. His efforts and those of other convicts and pardoned convicts in fields as diverse as engineering, architecture, commerce and the trades contributed substantially to the shaping of Tasmania as it is today.

Others who left their mark included artists Thomas Bock, Knut Bull and Thomas Wainewright, architect James Blackburn and sculptor Daniel Herbert.

Thomas Bock, an engraver and miniature-painter, was tried in 1823 for "administering drugs to produce abortion in a young woman named Yates." He was sentenced to transportation for 14 years and, on arrival, became an assigned servant of Dr E.F. Bromley. Bock's early work included the production of an engraved plate for a bank note of the Bank of Van Diemen's Land. He received

Ross Bridge over the Macquarie River is noted for its sculptures

▲▲ *"Manalargenna, A Chief of the Eastern Coast of VDL" by Thomas Bock (From the collection of the Tasmanian Museum and Art Gallery)*

▲ *Stone roller at Tunbridge was used by convict road gangs*

a free pardon in 1833 and went on to develop his talents as a portrait painter, becoming the first person to successfully practise this form of art professionally in Tasmania.

Bock was one of the few people to paint Aborigines from life before their lifestyles changed after they made contact with new settlers. His portraits of Aborigines in Robinson's missionary party between 1829 and 1834 are held by the Tasmanian Museum and Art Gallery, the Pitt Rivers Museum, Oxford, and the Royal Anthropological Institute, London.

After 30 years in Hobart Town, Bock died in 1855. His obituary in the "Hobart Town Courier" stated: *"He leaves a widow and a large family, we fear not too well provided for as Art is not yet sufficiently appreciated in these colonies to enrich its professors."*

Knut Bull, a convicted forger, was transported to Norfolk Island in 1846 and then to Tasmania a year later. Most of his time in Hobart was spent on assignment, with the Reverend J.G. Medland, an artist, among his masters. Bull's views of Hobart Town are his most noted works, examples of which were exhibited in the Paris Exposition of 1855, the Launceston Mechanics Institute Exhibition in 1860 and an "Old Hobart" Exhibition in 1896. After 10 years in Tasmania, Bull, who was also a portrait painter, left for New South Wales, where he died in 1889. There are examples of his work in the Tasmanian Museum and Art Gallery, "Narryna" and the Crowther Library.

Thomas Griffiths Wainewright had a colourful life, with art study, army service and journalism among his earlier pursuits. He went from being an exhibitor with the Royal Academy in 1821, 1824 and 1825 to the ranks of transportees bound for the colonies after he was convicted of forgery and uttering. Following his arrival in Hobart in 1837, Wainewright worked on a road chain-gang and as a hospital wardsman before becoming a sought-after portrait painter, working under the watchful eye of a guard. He was granted a conditional pardon in 1846 but died the following year.

Artistry of another kind was demonstrated by former highwayman Daniel Herbert and burglar James Colbeck. They were overseers for the construction of the Ross Bridge, which began in 1833. Colbeck was the master mason and Herbert did most of the intricate carvings of faces, animals and Celtic symbols that decorate 186 panels on the bridge arches. Both men earned their freedom as a result of their input to this project. St Luke's Church, Bothwell, also has carvings believed to be done by Herbert.

A number of fine colonial buildings, especially churches, were designed by James Blackburn, a gifted civil engineer, surveyor and architect. He was assigned to various government departments between 1833 and 1839, when he was pardoned and established a private practice. A short time later he moved to Campbell Town, where he was also involved in flour-milling, before finally settling in Melbourne in 1849. Blackburn was the architect

▶
"Blandfordia punicea" by William Buelow Gould (From the collection of Queen Victoria Museum and Art Gallery)

▶▶
St Mark' Church, Pontville

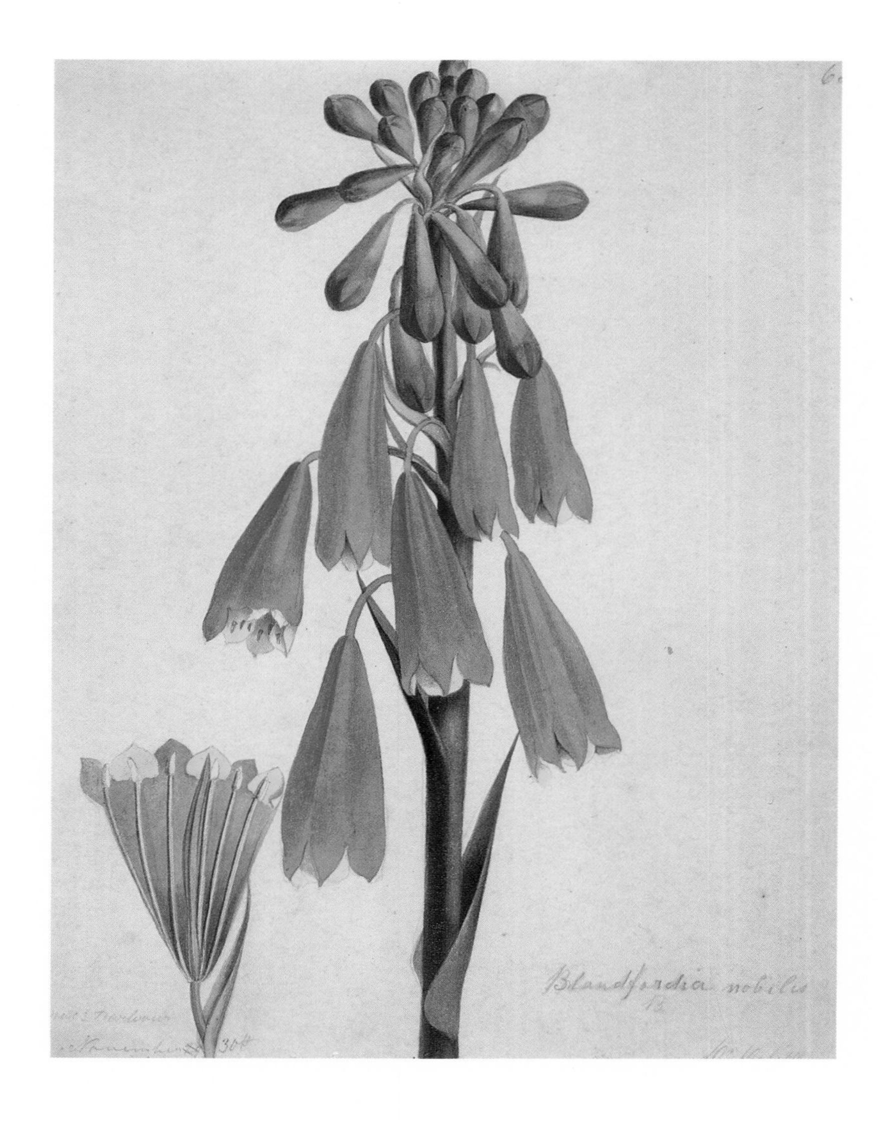

for a number of Campbell Town buildings, including The Grange, dating back to 1840. It is now used by the Adult Education Department, but this is not the first time The Grange has served to enlighten visitors. In 1874, astronomers travelled from near and far to view the transit of Venus from an observatory in the building.

Holy Trinity Church, Hobart, is among Blackburn's finest church designs, the foundation stone being laid by Tasmania's fifth Lieutenant-Governor, Sir John Franklin. The church has the oldest peal of bells in Australia. First rung on Regatta Day in 1847, the bells were restored in Britain as a bicentennial gift to Australia in 1988.

Sir John's wife, Jane, initiated and sponsored the development of another building designed by Blackburn, a Grecian-style museum at "Acanthe", Lenah Valley. Established in 1843, this was Australia's first public museum. It was planned to also use the building as a cultural centre, but it was decided later that this was not appropriate in a convict-based society. Ultimately, Lady Franklin's wishes have been fulfilled, with the premises serving as the Lady Franklin Gallery and a base for members of the Art Society of Tasmania.

Blackburn was also responsible for the design of St Mark's Church at Pontville, a Romanesque-style structure of local white ashlar stone. It is more than 150 years old and the graveyard at the rear provides a record of families associated with the area's development. The four-level tower of St George's Church at Battery Point, considered to be Australia's finest Greek Revival tower, is further proof of Blackburn's talents.

By the middle of the 19th century half of Tasmania's population were convicts or freed convicts. It was not until about the 1880s, when newcomers with no experience of the penal settlements began to gain wealth and power, that the gulf between people with "convict blood" and those of superior classes started to narrow. Numerous attempts were made to erase reminders of the past, such as changing the name of Port Arthur to Carnarvon towards the end of the century, and recycling building materials from places like the "Cascades" outstation. However, Port Arthur's title was reinstated in 1930 and gradually people became more curious about the State's convict heritage. A convict "past" was once best forgotten - now thousands of Tasmanians are proud to name convicts among their ancestors.

Port Arthur has been a leading Tasmanian visitor attraction since early this century and its buildings and their environs have been the subject of extensive archaeological excavation, preservation and restoration funded by the Commonwealth

◀
Port Arthur penitentiary

and State Governments since the late 1970s.

A classified historic site, it is managed by the Port Arthur Historic Site Management Authority, which is a statutory authority.

The major buildings include the asylum, a model prison, the Commandant's House and smaller cottages that were occupied by officials, while ruins such as those of the penitentiary, the guard house, the church and hospital help to build up a picture of what life was like here during its days as a penal settlement.

Across the bay, the Isle of the Dead was the final landfall for nearly 2,000 of the detainees, free settlers, soldiers, officials and their family members. Convicts were buried in communal graves but the inscriptions on headstones of other who died at Port Arthur contribute to the records.

Extensive bushfires in 1877 destroyed many buildings but it is still possible to visit the model prison, which was the subject of conservation work in the 1960s, and the recently refurbished asylum, now a visitor reception and education centre. The model prison was built in 1848 as an experiment in replacing use of the lash with a silent system of punishment for the incorrigibles. It had 50 cells initially, but this number was later increased to 68. Among the 12 solitary confinement cells were two that were soundproof and totally dark. A similar cell existed in a block at the "Cascades" outstation at Koonya, while some of the cells at the Saltwater River station were built in the coal mine galleries. Solitary confinement underground served as punishment for prisoners who continued to break the rules.

The solitary theme continued in the chapel at Port Arthur, where stalls were placed in such a way that convicts could not see each other. This chapel was restored in 1974. The four-storey

▲ *Ruins of the church*

◀◀
Asylum

◀
Penitentiary

◀◀
Turret of the guardhouse

◀
Prison exercise yard

▲▲
Accountant's house

▲
Roman Catholic chaplain's house

▶
Avenue of trees

▲
Cottage once used by Irish exile Smith O'Brien

▲▲ *Tranquility amidst ruggedness*

▲ *Headstones on the Isle of the Dead*

penitentiary, which was originally a granary and mill, had tiny cells on the first two floors for the worst offenders and other convicts slept in dormitories on the fourth floor. The mess hall was located on the third floor. These days, the penitentiary and the church are Port Arthur's most famous landmarks. The church, with its 13 spires representing Christ and His apostles, is believed to have been designed by James Blackburn. Construction began in 1834 and Governor Arthur laid the foundation stone two years later. A steeple that once formed part of the building was blown down in 1875. The church was never consecrated because it was used by several denominations.

The circular lookout tower of the guardhouse, built in 1835, was manned by those keeping watch on the settlement, including the now-demolished soldiers' quarters. There is evidence of other barracks at Salwater River, where an intricately carved doorway is among the ruins.

Near the guardhouse is the Commandant's House, the first section of which was built for Captain Charles O'Hara Booth in the 1830's. Set behind impressive timber gates and a sandstone wall, it is notable, in particular, for unusual wall paintings on either side of the verandah. The origin of the works, which feature the Parthenon and a dismasted ship, is unknown but it has been suggested that they may have been painted when this became the Carnarvon Hotel in the 1880s.

The Georgian residences of the Roman Catholic chaplain and the junior medical officer were restored in the 1980s, while the convict hospital at the former "Cascades" station is also proving useful once again - as colonial-style accommodation. The stone-floored morgue is excluded! An unusual carved stone pillar at the front of the former hospital is thought to have been part of the chapel font at "Cascaeds".

Officers' quarters and the overseer's cottage have also been restored at this settlement, where prisoners involved in timber-harvesting and milling often worked in irons weighing up to 40 pounds. It is still possible to follow the route of a tramway that ran up the valley for a mile from the bay to the forests where they worked.

At Taranna, there are reminders of other endeavours. The Norfolk Bay convict station, later an inn, a post office, art galleries and an accommodation house, was the northern terminus for a convict-propelled railway that ran seven kilometres to Long Bay. Three or four convicts harnessed to a carriage containing passengers and supplies pushed the vehicle up the hills and jumped on going downhill. The remains of this railway - the first in Australia - can be traced through the bush.

The eight major historic sites of the Tasman Peninsula all bear the scars of activities associated with the penal settlements. Time and nature have combined to wipe out many of the traces but Port Arthur remains as a part of Australia's living history.

Wagners
Cottage

Architecture

▲ *Gothic-Revival residence and Victorian Classical office of the Launceston Gas Company*

◀ *Wagner's Cottage, Swansea*

Tasmania's isolation is reflected in its architecture. This island of small settlements retains more of its 19th century and early 20th century streetscapes than most other places in Australia and it has not been subjected to the same development pressures and building booms experienced on the mainland.

The two eras of particular architectural significance are the colonial period, with older examples than in most parts of Australia, and the late 1970s and 1980s. The latter stage was marked by a breaking away from austere, functional modernism, which was still a leading force in other States, to produce small-scale, decorative buildings that harmonise with their surroundings. The Department of Veterans' Affairs centre in Davey Street, Hobart, the Rokeby fire station and the Bungawitta Child Care Centre in Launceston are among examples. By contrast, the Australian Antarctic Division headquarters at Kingston, which is also a commendable building of the period, is quite severe.

In general, Tasmanian architecture tends to be conservative, but notable exceptions occurred in the late 1930s and 1940s, when the State experienced its first taste of streamlined, modern styling. The leading exponent was architect Sydney Blythe, whose designs included the Ogilvie High School, Hobart, the Health Department building on the corner of Murray and Davey Streets, Hobart, and the Queenstown High School. They feature horizontal lines, with long bands of metal-framed windows, curved corners and circular stairwells, and were progressive in terms of both planning and utility.

Another significant project that was started soon after it was first mooted in 1920 was the establishment of the Cadbury's Estate at Claremont. This is one of the few Garden City developments outside England, the aim being to provide factory workers with some of the advantages of country life. The initial layout of winding streets, parklands and a recreation oval was the work of William John Earle, of Adelaide, but Hobart architect Bernard Walker was responsible for the houses, which he described as "gardeners' cottages." The Cadbury Schweppes company still owns the factory site but the estate was broken up in the early 1970s.

On a different scale, Walker also designed a number of the black sump oil-stained vertical board cottages with brick bases that are found in places like Fern Tree and the old holiday home area of Kingston Beach.

One of the first people to influence urban design in Tasmania was Governor Lachlan

▲
Officers' quarters and mess, Anglesea Barracks

Macquarie, whose initial visit from New South Wales in 1811 was followed by a second trip in 1821. Confronted with rows of slab huts that had replaced the tents of the early settlements, Macquarie directed that new buildings should be of brick or stone construction. He initiated improvements to the layout of Hobart and named its major streets - Macquarie, Liverpool, Argyle, Elizabeth, Murray, Harrington and Collins Streets. Travelling north, he continued to bestow names - Macquarie Springs, York Plains, Campbell Town Epping Forest...

The island remained a dependent of the Colony of New South Wales until 1825 and the security of the southern settlement was the responsibility of a detachment of troops from Macquarie's Regiment, the 73rd of Foot. During his first visit to Hobart, Macquarie expressed concern about the accommodation provided for the troops and directed that barracks be built on a small hill just south-west of the town centre. The Anglesea Barracks complex, which is the headquarters of the Australian Army and the Royal Australian Navy in Tasmania, is now the oldest military establishment in the nation that is still occupied by the Army.

The original officers' quarters and mess, the foundation stone of which was laid in 1814, was restored in 1970 and serves as the current officers' mess and quarters for unmarried officers. Wrought iron fittings, chandeliers and wallpaper in Georgian patterns are featured inside the building, which was erected in three stages, and Regency-style fanlights, original Huon pine flooring indoors and flagging on the verandah have been preserved. Another impressive building is the gaol, erected in 1846 from locally quarried freestone. Its heavily studded doors, elegant stone pillars and carved window lintels create an imposing picture that contrasts with the sombre scene in the block of 13 cells. A 6th Military District Museum was established in the gaol in 1985, its contents including the Cameron Collection, which consists of uniforms, medals, a hip bath, a stretcher and even a pantaloon press that belonged to members of the Cameron family, pioneers of the Nile area in 1820. Among the Camerons' famous "military sons" was Cyril St Clair Cameron, who led the first Tasmanian contingent to the Boer War and was elected by Tasmania to the first Australian Senate. He was later instrumental in the formation of the Royal Australian Navy.

Two memorials at the Barracks also form part of Tasmania's heritage. A stone archway that once graced the Bath Inn on the Midland Highway now marks the entrance to a memorial corner where there is a 99th Regiment Memorial and a commemorative wall with 22 military gravestones. A contingent of troops from the regiment, which was stationed in Hobart from 1845 to 1856, was sent to New Zealand to fight in the Maori Wars and this is the only memorial erected in Australia by a British regiment to commemorate members who were killed while on active service. The second remembrance monument dates from more recent times. It was constructed in 1967 from

▲▲
Gunpowder magazine, Queen's Domain

▲
Bluff Battery, Bellerive

stone removed from buildings burnt out in disastrous bushfires that swept southern Tasmania in February that year, resulting in the deaths of 62 people. The monument commemorates the rescue efforts of both regular and civilian soldiers of Anglesea Barracks.

Launceston also lists barracks among its oldest buildings. The Paterson Barracks in St John Street were built in 1827 as a commissariat store, the Commissariat Corps being part of the defence system at that time. The building is still occupied by the Army and is the base for the 16 Field Battery and a detachment of 10 Field Ambulance.

Other examples of military architecture are found in a series of batteries on the Hobart foreshore and in associated buildings such as the sandstone gunpowder magazine on the Queen's Domain. This magazine, which was built by convicts in the early 1850s, still retains its interior fittings, including copper-sheathed doors, oregon shelves and bronze and copper air locks and vents. The Queen's Battery is on the Domain, while the Alexandra Battery overlooks the river at Sandy Bay, the Bellerive Bluff Battery is on the eastern shore and the Mulgrave Battery, which dates from 1818, forms part of Princes Park, Battery Point. Underground chambers that were built to store ammunition and other supplies for the guns of the Mulgrave Battery are a prime visitor attraction in Battery Point, an historic suburb named after this battery of guns.

It was fear of war with Russia in the 1880s that led to the establishment of the Queens, Bluff and Alexandra batteries, the trenches and massive stone walls of the latter two remaining visible. A short time later, an ammunition depot was built near the mouth of the River Derwent at Fort Direction, now a training area as well as a depot.

All British garrison troops had been withdrawn from Tasmania by 1870, with volunteer regiments forming the bulk of the military force until Federation, when the responsibility for defence passed from the former colonial governments to the Commonwealth of Australia.

By then, nearly 100 years had passed since Europeans settled in Tasmania, the initial battle for survival being followed by a golden age of building between 1820 and 1840, economic depression in the 1840s, growth in agricultural and mining industries and further depression in the 1890s. The 19th century buildings, bridges and other structures that remain reflect these "highs" and "lows."

With most early settlers coming from Britain, houses and furniture were often simplified versions of those they had left behind. Buildings were well-proportioned, with a colonial effect resulting from the addition of verandahs that extended from under the main roof - a concession to the Australian heat. The Georgian architectural form remained dominant in Tasmania until the 1850s - about 20 years longer than in Britain. It was followed by Victorian, Federation and, later, Picturesque (influenced by the arts and crafts movement in England), Art Deco (including the use of abstract geometric patterns), Modern and Post-Modern styles.

Hobart, proclaimed a city in 1842, is generally considered Australia's most historic capital in terms of its buildings and atmosphere, while Launceston, which became a city in 1888, has been less affected by modern intrusions and retains a Victorian image that is of special value in terms of Australian heritage. The other cities are Glenorchy, Burnie, Devonport and Clarence.

The central part of Launceston remains virtually intact, with recycling of old buildings and the development of the quaint, curved Quadrant Mall adding to the city's character. Rows of terrace houses, small wooden cottages in Inveresk and other old suburbs, well-preserved commercial premises, imposing churches and extensive public parks and gardens have all contributed to the face of Launceston.

St John's Church, in the street of the same name, is one of the oldest buildings. Its construction began in 1824, with further additions to the brick, sandstone and concrete structure at the beginning of this century and in 1938. St John's overlooks Princes Square, where political meetings were held early last century before the area was used as a brick field. This Victorian-style park, developed in the 1850s to the design of Thomas Wade, features gracious old trees, including an oak planted in 1868 by the then Duke of Edinburgh. The central bronze fountain, which was bought at the Paris Exhibition of 1858, was originally topped by a provocative nymph, but staid Victorian attitudes resulted in this being replaced with a pineapple on arrival in Tasmania! The fountain commemorates the first water supply system in Launceston, with a nearby drinking fountain, erected in 1866, demonstrating the connection in an even more a more tangible way.

Another recreation area, City Park, is almost as old as Launceston, itself. The residence of the northern Lieutenant-Governor used to be here, and the park, which covers about five hectares, was developed in the late 1820s. At its edge is the Albert Hall, an exhibition building in the High Victorian Classical style. Built in 1891 for the Tasmanian International Exhibition at a cost of £12,000 the hall features an unusual tower with a gilded ball finial. Inside, a Brindley water organ, which was imported from England in 1861 and was originally installed in the Mechanics' Institute, Launceston, has pride of place by the stage. The oldest civic organ in Australia, it was extensively restored in 1980.

Launceston's title of the "Garden City" is well-deserved and is due in no small part to the preservation of gardens at the Cataract Gorge and Cliff Grounds. The Cliff Gardens were developed at the turn of this century, with the Launceston City Council embarking on a major restoration and upgrading program in 1974. The work included rehabilitation of the Victorian band rotunda, the tearooms and Gorge cottage and reconstruction of a toll house. It's a far cry from the early days of settlement when the nearby First Basin was the main washing place of the town!

Brisbane Street has always been Launceston's main retail area, the Georgian facades of many buildings being replaced by Victorian finishes after the discovery of tin at Mt Bischoff in 1871 increased the fortunes of a considerable number of Launceston businessmen. The change from simple to more-ostentatious styling was a demonstration of their new-found wealth.

A short distance away from Brisbane Street, the Post Office clock, installed to celebrate the centenary of settlement, maintains its role of more than 85 years in ringing out the time from its lofty tower, while century-old churches, like the Paterson Street Uniting Church, chime their summonses to followers. Not all of Launceston's historic gems are large structures, however. The retention of items such as a red pillar box outside the Queen Victoria Museum and Art Gallery, the oldest functional letterbox in Tasmania, and the Adye Douglas Fountain, a focal point at the intersection of Elphin Road and High Street, also contribute to the streetscapes. The fountain, which originally incorporated a street lamp, was used for watering horses and dogs.

Unlike many places, the needs of expansion in Launceston have been met, to a large extent, by recycling, rather than building anew. The Crown Mill, which began operation in 1898 as a flour mill and has now taken on a new lease of life as professional offices, was the subject of a major conversion that was completed in 1979. This project has been followed by similar undertakings, including the creation of an Art Centre for the Launceston College of Technical and Further Education in the former Thynes Knitting Mill in York Street, used in earlier times by the Union Brewery, and the recycling of an 1888 warehouse known as the Murray Building, which now houses professional offices. The role of the Colonial Motor Inn has also changed significantly since the days when it rang out to the sounds of schoolboys attending the Launceston Grammar School here in the mid-19th century.

The restoration of former abattoir workers' cottages in Balfour Street, also for visitor accommodation, has helped to ensure that simple buildings of the past are preserved along with the grander residences and public premises.

The same situation applies in many areas of Tasmania as the owners of historic properties ranging from bakeries to barns, a gaolhouse and a convict hospital open up the buildings to enable travellers to share in this heritage.

Since the 1960s, the National Trust, Tasmania, has been the main "guardian" of the State's historic properties. This has occurred as a result of Trust ownership and through its classification and recording of buildings and other structures that warrant preservation because they form part of

▲▲
Dunorlan Cottages, Launceston, were built as almshouses to accommodate destitute women

▲▶
Italienate terrace in St John Street dates back to the 1880s

▲
Albert Hall

▲
The finely decorated Joseph's Corner Shops occupy a focal point in Brisbane Street

▶
Thynes Mill tower in York Street exemplifies an Edwardian industrial mill building

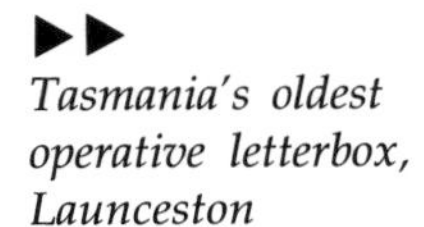

▶▶
Tasmania's oldest operative letterbox, Launceston

Tasmania's history or have architectural significance.

The initial instigators for the formation of a National Trust branch in Tasmania were Launceston couples, Dr and Mrs Clifford Craig and Mr and Mrs R.M. Green, whose actions were motivated by a desire to acquire and preserve "The Hollies", a Georgian-style house at Franklin Village. A branch of the Trust was subsequently founded in Launceston and "The Hollies", now known as "Franklin House", became the Trust's first property in Tasmania.

Within three years, Regional Committees had been formed in southern and north-western centres and, nowadays, Trust Groups, which are sub-committees of the three Regional Committees, are active in most parts of the island. Additional support for the members' work included an appeal conducted nationally by the National Trust (Australia) to raise funds for the acquisition and restoration of the Wybalenna chapel on Flinders island, which was built during the period of Aboriginal re-settlement, between 1833 and 1847. For a number of years before its restoration, the simple Georgian chapel, with its timber floors and slate roof, was used as a shearing shed. Even when it is surrounded by a profusion of Spring bulbs it still evokes a lonesome feeling - a link perhaps with its past...

In addition to mansions like "Clarendon" at Nile, "Entally", Hadspen, and "Runnymede", Hobart, the Trust is also responsible for a variety of places that have figured in commercial and political history and, in the case of the Penitentiary Chapel and Criminal Courts, Hobart, the development of the penal system. The Old Umbrella Shop, Launceston, and the Callington Mill, Oatlands, are among the properties that have housed commercial and industrial operations.

"Franklin House" was built in 1838 for Launceston brewer and innkeeper, Britton Jones, but just four years later it became a "Classical and Commercial School" run by William Keeler Hawkes. It cost 45 guineas a year for young gentlemen to attend the school, where the subjects included Greek, Latin, Logic and Rhetoric. The original cedar woodwork of doors, architraves, mantlepieces and shutter interiors is one of the building's most outstanding features.

"Clarendon", situated 27 kilometres from Launceston on the banks of the South Esk River, is the jewel in the Trust's crown. One of Australia's great Georgian houses, it was completed in 1838 for James Cox, a wealthy woolgrower and merchant, and was donated to the Trust in 1962 by a later owner, Mrs W.R. Menzies. Work undertaken during an extensive restoration program, which began in 1964, included the re-establishment of the portico - an unusual inclusion in a domestic property of the colonial period. The purchase in 1987 of outbuildings used previously by servants and farm workers has facilitated the

▲
"Clarendon", Nile

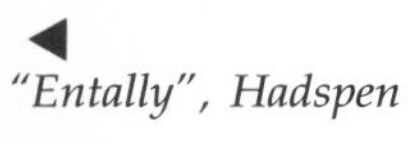

◀
"Entally", Hadspen

Blackwood is used extensively in the Old Umbrella Shop

"Franklin House"

▶
Penitentiary Chapel, Hobart

presentation of a total picture of life "upstairs" and "downstairs".

"Entally", named after a suburb of Calcutta, India, is among Tasmania's oldest houses. It was established in 1819 by Thomas Reibey, whose son was one of Tasmania's early Premiers. Stone stables, a two-storey brick coach-house, a bluestone chapel and cottage are among the fascinating outbuildings. Entry to the house is by way of a four-panel front door with half sidelights and a radial fanlight, an important feature of colonial architecture because these creations, often carved from a single piece of cedar or other timber, represented domestic pride. The property was bought by the State Government in 1948 and is leased to the National Trust.

Regency-style "Runnymede", in Hobart's oldest suburb, New Town, has had a number of interesting owners - and name changes - since it was built in 1836 for Robert Pitcairn, who called it "Cairn Lodge". Pitcairn, the first lawyer to qualify in the colony and a leading advocate for the abolition of transportation, sold the house in 1850 to the Right Reverend Francis Russell Nixon, the first Anglican Bishop in Van Diemen's Land. The property was re-named "Bishopstowe" and gardens were planted by Mrs Nixon, who wanted to create an English-style haven. There was a further name change when a seafarer, Captain Charles Bayley, bought the house in 1864 and called it "Runnymede", after his favourite ship. The property, which is noted for the fine timber trellis work on the verandah, its elegant music room and period furnishings, remained with Bayley's descendants until it was sold to the State Government in 1957.

"Runnymede" is leased by the National Trust, as is the Penitentiary Chapel and Criminal Courts complex, set behind lovely mature trees on the corner of Campbell and Brisbane Streets, Hobart. This is the southern headquarters for the Trust - a totally different use from that envisaged by architect John Lee Archer when he designed the buildings! They were completed in 1834 and are one of Australia's better known examples of Georgian ecclesiastical architecture. This was the church and gaol offices of the original Hobart Gaol, with two of the wings being converted in 1860 for use as criminal courts, a situation that remained unchanged until 1983. Services were held in the chapel, a feature of which is the Corinthian clocktower, up until 1961.

Contrasting with this large complex, complete with its underground passages and cells, is the tiny Old Umbrella Shop, which houses the National Trust Gift Shop and Information Centre in George Street, Launceston. Built in the 1860s, this is the last genuine period shop in Tasmania, with three generations of the Schott family having operated the blackwood-lined store since the turn of this century. They specialised in umbrellas and walking sticks, a selection of which is still on display.

Unlike the pristine umbrella shop, the Callington Mill at Oatlands, in the Midlands, had fallen into disrepair over the years. Now, however, largely as a result of renewed interest and funds generated during Australia's bicentenary year, the 1837 flour mill is being restored to its former glory. It is one of the oldest mills in Australia, providing a rare example of a bygone industrial era. The final stage of the restoration by the National Trust

▶
Lyon's Cottage, Stanley

involves re-fitting huge sails atop the mill tower, the stones of which are tapered, with each course curved to a different arc.

The diversified interests of the Trust include ownership of the contents of "Home Hill", once the Devonport home of former Australian Prime Minister Joseph Lyons and Dame Enid Lyons. The single-storey timber house and landscaped grounds belong to the City of Devonport. Another residence of Joseph Lyons is also open to the public. It's a tiny timber cottage in which he was born at Stanley in 1879. The cottage dates back to the 1840s and is agood example of a weatherboard dwelling of this period. During his time as Premier of Tasmania, Lyons and his wife lived in a house they bought in New Town Road, Hobart.

▶▶
"Runnymede", New Town, with views of dining room, study and fine trellis work on verandah

Joseph Lyons was Premier from 1923 to 1928, after which he entered Federal politics. He is the only Tasmanian to have been Prime Minister (from 1932 until 1939) and the only Australian to serve as a State Premier as well as Prime Minister. Dame Enid also had an outstanding parliamentary career. In 1943 she became the first woman member of the House of Representatives and in 1949 she was sworn in as the first woman Federal Minister of the Crown.

Contributions to heritage through government come not only in the form of people, but also in property. A most outstanding example is Tasmania's Government House, which novelist Anthony Trollope described in 1873 as "the best Government House in any British colony", adding that it "lacks for nothing necessary for a perfect English residence."

"Home Hill", Devonport, was also a residence of Joseph Lyons

The gardens of the 10-hectare parkland surrounding the Gothic Revival vice-regal residence are equally impressive. Ornamental pools were created in former quarries that were the source of brown sandstone used in the walls of the building and white sandstone for the quoins. Gardens were established here long before Tasmania's third Government House was erected on the site that had been selected by Governor Arthur in 1824. Much of the area that was worked by gardeners in the 1830s now forms part of the adjoining Royal Tasmanian Botantical Gardens.

Government House was a long time in the making, but the finished product, which cost £67,000 to build and utilised the services of the best masons and craftsmen, was well worth the wait. First mooted by Governor Macquarie in 1811, Government House was not completed until 1858, earlier official residences being a three-roomed dwelling occupied by Lieutenant-Governor Collins and a 14-roomed house built in 1817 between the present-day sites of the Town Hall and Franklin Square. The second building was rickety, draughty and most uncomfortable, with the Governor's guests often lodging with his wealthy friends. With the exception of the ballroom, which was used from time to time as a meeting place of the local council, the forerunner of today's Government House was demolished on completion of the new building.

After numerous delays and the submission of varied plans, including those of government architect John Lee Archer and ex-convict architect James Blackburn, William Porden Kay, a nephew of Governor Franklin's wife, was selected to design Government House.

There are two main entrances, one for pedestrians and the other intended for visitors arriving by coach. The first is at the foot of a tall octagonal tower that faces west, while the other is by way of an imposing door sheltered by a porte-cochere, which is set in a larger clocktower. A stone carving at the top of the pedestrians' entrance depicts the establishment of the colony.

Other important sculptures with an even longer history are found on the river-side of the house. A large stone rosette set in a wall near the solarium, created by extending the original conservatory,

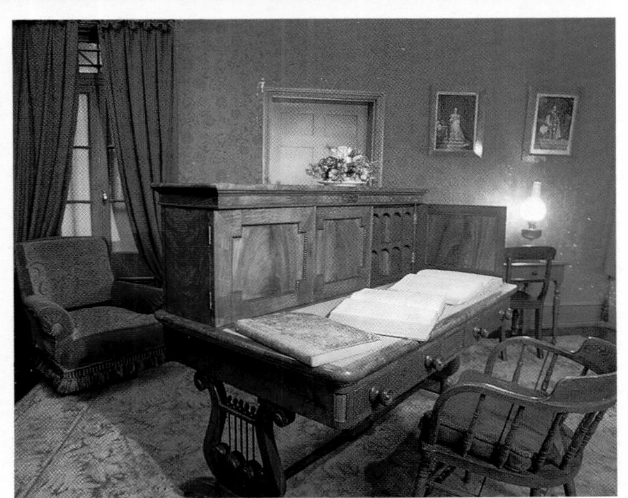

and a lion's head above the adjacent schoolroom door were sculpted in the 15th century and formed part of Britain's House of Lords. They were brought to Tasmania by Sir Ernest Clark, who was Governor from 1933 to 1945. No expense was spared in furnishing Government House, with many of the custom-made fittings and furniture, such as dining chairs, still in use today. The strong patterns and colours of Victorian decorating have been retained, with an ecclesiastical influence in the ballroom, which was built as a separate wing and opens off the drawing room. Huge crystal chandeliers hang from the high vaulted ceiling, a musicians' gallery having a full view to the other end of the room, where there is a dais for investitures.

The public rooms are all at ground level, while the Governor's private apartment and suites of rooms for house guests are on the first floor.

In recent times, Government House has been opened to the public on a number of occasions, enabling the community to gain a greater appreciation of this architectural treasure of world standing.

Standing stately on a main approach to Hobart, Government House sets the scene for a city that successfully combines the past and the present. This aspect is illustrated well in Sullivans Cove, with the Sullivans Cove Development Authority - an advisory body funded by the State Government, the Marine Board of Hobart and the Hobart City Council - helping to revitalise and increase appreciation of the area. Modern structures like the CSIRO Marine Laboratories in Castray Esplanade harmonise with the nearby mellowed sandstone warehouses that line Salamanca Place and include the best group of waterfront Georgian warehouses in Australia. Built between 1835 and

Views of Government House, including the two main entrances and carvings above the pedestrians' entrance, depicting the colony's establishment, and in an exterior wall

1860 on a level area created by quarrying, the warehouses originally fronted directly on to the New Wharf and were the centre for trade and commerce in Hobart. Many of the three and four-storey sandstone buildings are now important bases of another kind - the headquarters of a number of organisations and individuals involved in the production, promotion and sale of Tasmanian art and crafts. The Saturday morning market, first held on the pavement and roadway of Salamanca Place about 20 years ago, is now an integral part of the city's culture.

The warehouses here complement a row of buildings on the other side of the cove, adjoining the Old Wharf. Featuring arched goods entries and Georgian-style windows, the Old Wharf complex dates from 1826 and served for more than 60 years as the headquarters of the Henry Jones IXL jam factory and fruit canning business from early this century. The occupants nowadays include restaurants, government departments and the University of Tasmania's Centre for the Arts. The success of the conversion of this Centre, with modifications revealing much of the former factory skeleton, was recognised in 1987 when the project received the National Award for Recycled Buildings in the annual Royal Australian Institute of Architects' Awards.

As in Launceston, recycling is becoming a more common practise for designers and developers, with modern buildings that have become obsolete being among the subjects. The conversion of a service station in Murray Street into a streamlined centre housing the Hobart Animal Hospital is one such example. On the other hand, some service stations have achieved merit in their own right... A quaint little station in Victoria Street, complete with a Roman canopy supported by Classical columns, epitomises the style of pre-World War 11 establishments of this kind.

Other buildings to make their mark this century include Hobart's first multi-storey office block, the Commonwealth Bank, on the corner of Elizabeth and Liverpool Streets, which stood out on the city skyline when it was completed in 1954, and a soaring complex of another kind - the Wrest Point Hotel-Casino, designed by Sir Roy Grounds and featuring a 17-storey tower that creates a harbourside landmark at Sandy Bay. The upward trend continued in the 1970s with the establishment of such buildings as the SBT Bank in Murray Street. On a different scale, and important as a trendsetter, the Rokeby fire station, on the eastern shore, has achieved national and international recognition for the way in which it combines a functional design with a "fun image." In many ways, this station, designed by the firm of Howroyd and Forward in 1979, marked the advent of Post-Modernism in Tasmania.

Development of the Cat and Fiddle Arcade in 1960 also brightened the Hobart scene. This was the first significant attempt to incorporate old and

▲ *Salamanca Place buildings have taken on new roles*

Wrestpoint Drawing ▲

◀ *Wrest Point Hotel-Casino*

▼ *St David's Cathedral*

▶▲
Awaiting recycling - a former townhouse of Henry Jones in the IXL complex

▲
Original fittings have been retained in the conversion of another section that is now headquarters of Tasmanian Sea Fisheries

▼
Rokeby Fire Station

new work. Ramshackle timber houses for up to 200 people lined this warehouse and service alley last century. Its transformation into pedestrian walks, retail shopping areas and a square featuring an animated clockwork rendition of the famous Cat and Fiddle nursery rhyme has made this one of Hobart's most popular open spaces.

Much of today's architecture will become the heritage of tomorrow, but it's often easier to recognise the value of works once a reasonable period of time has elapsed and the structures can be viewed in the overall context of the era in which they were created. As a result, greater emphasis is often placed on the merits of older buildings. In the case of Hobart, however, there is justification for such a stance as the city has many of Australia's finest colonial homes and public properties. Their worth was appreciated as far back as 1833, when the following excerpt appeared in "The Hobart Town Monthly Magazine":

"Although we are fair to confess that there is plenty of room for Hobart Town architectural innovations and improvements, still, all things considered, it is a very surprising town. It has good shops, excellent inns, with excellent prices, a commodious church, with a very ***in****-commodious steeple, and several buildings of*

▲
Hobart Synagogue

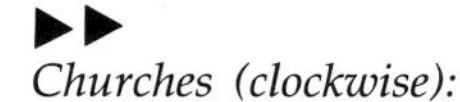
Churches (clockwise):

The Church of St John the Baptist at Buckland has a stained glass window that is said to have been designed for Battle Abbey, built on the site of the Battle of Hastings

St Peter's, Oatlands

Uniting Church, Fingal

St James' Church, Ranelagh

Uniting Church, Ross

St Mark's, Deloraine

St Matthew's, Pontville

character by no means conspicuous for elegance, while its inhabitants are computed in the aggregate at eight thousand souls."

The church referred to was St David's, the second to record this name in the colony. The first one blew down in a storm after two years, with work on its successor beginning in 1817. The present St David's Cathedral dates back to 1868.

Churches have always played an important role in the community, as this report from the 1830 "Hobart Town Almanack and Van Diemen's Land Annual" indicates...

"The crowded and most respectacle congregation of this church, (St David's) *and the exemplary manner in which public workship is conducted, especially at the forenoon service, must agreeably surprise the stranger who after a voyage of four or five months lands in this remote, and till within a few years, wholly uncultivated region.*

The Presbyterian and Wesleyan chapels, both in Melville street (besides the Roman Catholic) are also neat buildings, and do credit to the town, not only as respectable structures, but also from the regular and orderly manner in which they are attended by their numerous congregations."

The Hobart Synagogue, set behind a railing fence in Argyle Street, is Australia's oldest place of Jewish worship. Dating back to 1843, it is an excellent example of a Regency Egyptian Revival building, as is the Launceston Synagogue, completed one year later. The land for Hobart's synagogue, which was designed by convict architect J.A. Thomson, was donated by Judah and Joseph Solomon, who also built the adjoining Temple House, completed in 1826. Along with Ingle Hall, built in 1814 on the corner of Argyle and Macquarie Streets, this is a rare example of a complete Georgian townhouse in Australia. Following extensive restoration, Temple Hall is to be incorporated in Tasmania Police headquarters.

In the early days of the colony most churches were erected by the Government or with government assistance, but this situation altered in the mid-1800s. Simpler designs were often chosen for churches and the inclusion of towers became virtually a thing of the past.

St Mary's Cathedral, the first section of which was finished in 1876, and nearby St Mary's College, St Virgil's College and the Archbishop's Palace in Barrack Street were all designed by Henry Hunter, one of Tasmania's most prolific Victorian architects. Hunter's "presence" is evident in the buildings of towns throughout the State, including the smaller centres of Ross, Campbell Town, Latrobe, Ouse

▲▲
One of the fine stone buildings at the intersection of Macquarie and Murray Streets

▲
Hobart Town Hall, designed by prolific architect Henry Hunter (Tasmaniana Library collection)

and Deloraine. Among his important projects were the Tasmanian Museum and Art Gallery, which was built in 1863 and features fine stone detailing, and the Hobart Town Hall, erected in three stages and completed in 1866. A box deposited when the foundation stone of the Town Hall was laid two years earlier contained coins of the day and copies of the four local newspapers.

The Town Hall is one of the major public buildings in Macquarie Street, a "starting point" for the city. As far back as 1831, when the following account was published in "A Statistical View of Van Diemen's Land" it was a main thoroughfare:

"Macquarie Street, in which most of the public buildings and offices are placed, runs along a sort of ridge or terrace, by a gentle ascent to upwards of a mile from the wharf, commanding on one side a beautiful prosperous town, backed with picturesque hills and distant mountains, and on the other a full view of the harbour and shipping."

Then, as now, the intersection of Macquarie and Murray Streets was a key element of Hobart. The scene was dominated by the high walls of the gaol, which had an underground tunnel linking it with the court house, built opposite in 1832. Police and convict offices were erected in 1837 and a central section, now occupied by the Treasury Department, was added in 1841. Public Buildings fronting Macquarie Street and Franklin Square date from the mid-1840s, with the former Supreme Court completing the complex of Victorian Classical Revival buildings in 1910.

Today, the intersection of Murray and Macquarie Streets presents one of the nation's finest examples of an early streetscape. The corners are occupied by the government-owned buildings, commercial premises and St David's Cathedral.

Farther down Murray Street is Parliament House, which was formerly the custom house. It is among the outstanding works of John Lee Archer, who was Colonial Architect for 11 years from 1828. His influence can be seen in many parts of the State - from Stanley to Low Head, Bothwell, Campbell Town, Ross and Richmond. He designed three churches that bear the name "St Luke's", as well as bridges, gaols, wharves, tombs, lighthouses and other government properties.

When Parliament House was part of the customs system the bonded cargo was held in underground vaults, which are now used to store parliamentary memorabilia. In 1851, Van Diemen's Land became the first colony to receive self-government and it was renamed Tasmania in 1856, coinciding with the opening of the first Parliament. The State still has two houses of parliament, the House of Assembly and the Legislative Council, which reviews legislation put forward by the House of Assembly.

St David's Park, which is opposite Parliament House, was the first burial ground for Hobart and a selection of early headstones are mounted in a memorial wall. There are also memorials to pioneers and others who contributed to the colony's

▲
Battery Point has a fascinating "mix" of architectural styles among its dwellings

▶
"Narryna" is now a museum

▶▶
Kelly's Steps still link Battery Point with Salamanca Place

▲
Battery Point: St George's Church and Arthur's Circus

advancement, including mariner James Kelly, who was appointed Harbourmaster and Pilot for the Derwent in 1819.

Kelly owned about 15 hectares of land in Battery Point, with Kelly Street being named after him in 1840. Sandstone steps built for him at this time to connect Sullivans Cove and the waterfront with the residential area of Battery Point are still used frequently today.

By 1850 Battery Point had become a mariners' village. A survey of 127 households in 1852 showed that 9 were occupied by master mariners, 10 by shipwrights, 3 each by coopers, boatbuilders and seamen, 1 each by a harbourmaster, water policeman, tide waiter, coxswain and fisherman, plus numerous shipping agents, merchants, clerks and men involved with slips or wharves. Battery Point still retains its village atmosphere and links with the sea, notably in the form of its slipways and marine engineering works.

Two architects were responsible for the design of an outstanding landmark, St George's Church, in Cromwell Street. The body of the building, completed in 1838, was designed by John Lee Archer, while the tower, which was added in 1847, is the work of architect James Blackburn. The adjoining Georgian building was originally a "poor school."

Arthur's Circus is another focal point, its single-storey brick cottages arranged around a central park having been built between 1847 and 1852 on land that once belonged to colonial chaplain the Reverend Robert Knopwood. It was acquired by Governor Arthur, who had it divided into 16 plots that were described as "delectable building sites" and subsequently sold for £40 each.

Among the more-substantial residences are "Lenna", which was erected for shipowner and merchant Alexander McGregor and is now a hotel, and "Narryna", an elegant Georgian house with a lovely fountain in gardens behind a front fence of stone and iron railings. "Narryna" houses a museum centred on social lifestyles of the 19th century, while "Secheron House", built in 1832 for Surveyor-General George Frankland, is also an historic display centre. It is the headquarters of the Maritime Museum of Tasmania. Cedar has been used extensively in the large rooms of "Secheron House", with views beyond the wide verandah to the River Derwent providing an ideal setting for the museum's unique collection of paintings, photographs, models, figureheads and other maritime artefacts.

Many of the 19th century inns of Battery Point and Salamanca Place still draw customers but the modern crowds are more moderate, in all respects, than the rowdy whalers and other seafarers who used to frequent these public houses.

Throughout the island, inns were frequently the first buildings of any substance in an area. The Main Road between Hobart and Launceston was dotted with "watering holes" that were conveniently placed to cater for travellers and the changing of stage coach horses. There were 40,000

▲▲
Stone horse trough, Melton Mowbray

▲
Shot Tower, Taroona, a roadside landmark

people in Tasmania in 1835 and they were serviced by 91 public houses in Hobart, 27 in Richmond and Sorell, 9 at New Norfolk, 4 in Oatlands and 93 in Launceston, the inland and the North-West.

The Red Feather Inn, Hadspen, Bonney's Inn, Deloraine, St Andrews Inn at Cleveland, the Scotch Thistle Inn, Ross, the Richmond Arms Hotel and the Batman Fawkner Inn, Launceston, whose first landlord, John Pascoe Fawkner, planned the early settlement of Melbourne, are among the survivors. At the Melton Mowbray Hotel, where the second landlord, Samuel Blackwell, had his own course for horseracing, a stone horse trough carved from one piece of stone has also stood the test of time. These establishments contrast with their ultra-modern counterparts like the Sheraton Hotel, the Launceston International and Launceston Federal and Wrest Point Hotel-Casino complexes.

A roadside landmark of a different kind, the Shot Tower at Taroona, is a monument to a pioneer of technology, Joseph Moir. With the assistance of two masons, he built the 66-metre tower in 1870, using more than 8,000 individually curved and tapered sandstone blocks. Molten lead was dropped from the top of the tower into water, where it formed spheres of shot. This was the first shot tower in Australia, but although it was a mechanical success the cost of raw materials was high and the venture proved to be a commercial failure.

One of the most striking things about Tasmania is the large number of communities where occupations and leisure pursuits have basically remained unaltered for more than a century. These places include the classified historic towns of Queenstown, which is still closely allied with the mining industry of the west coast, Stanley and Strahan, with their maritime links, and Swansea, Ross, Deloraine and Bothwell, which have serviced the surrounding rural areas since their foundation.

Tasmania has 17 officially classified historic towns: Evandale, Longford, Low Head, Oatlands, Ross, Swansea, Westbury, Bothwell, Hamilton, Kempton, New Norfolk, Richmond, Deloraine, Queenstown, Strahan, Zeehan and Stanley, with Battery Point a classified historic village.

Some centres have significant landmarks - the bridges of Ross and Richmond, the Gaiety Theatre in Zeehan and the Callington Mill at Oatlands, for instance, but generally it is the overall planning and architecture that sets Tasmania's historic towns apart from the newly established areas.

The predominance of certain types of building materials within regions has its roots in the days when local supplies were usually all that was available. The timber buildings of Huon and north-western centres, the freestone ones on the east coast, the sandstone structures in Oatlands, Pontville and Hobart and those of grey freestone in Ross provide such evidence.

Although it is not restricted to particular geographic areas, another feature of Tasmanian architecture is the use of Victorian iron lacework, and fretted turned timber verandah detailing and bargeboards. The timber was more readily

▲▲
Timber fretwork, Fingal cottage

▲
Verandah trellis, "Highfield"

▲▲
Pillar, St Peter's Church, Oatlands

▲
Victorian Classical dwelling, Westbury

◀
Dressed stone quoins, Baptist Church, Dysart

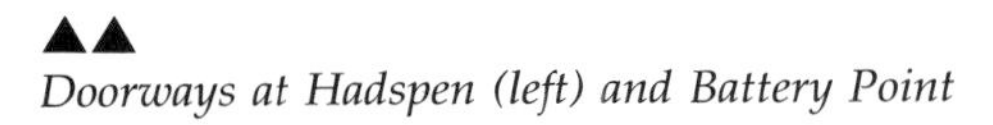

▲▲
Doorways at Hadspen (left) and Battery Point

▶
Verandah post bracket, St Mary's dwelling

▼
Rising sun fanlight on Georgian cottage, Oatlands

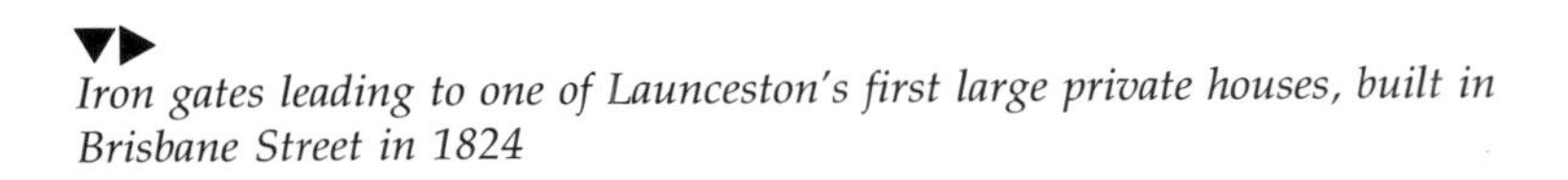

▼▶
Iron gates leading to one of Launceston's first large private houses, built in Brisbane Street in 1824

▲▲
Effective use of timber on house at Westbury and Bothwell guesthouse

Ornamental cast iron fence and gates, Launceston Showgrounds

▶
▶
Historic bridge, Richmond, with view to St John's Church

procurable than the iron but the lacework is found in many properties, nevertheless. It decorates hotels in Richmond, Cygnet, Queenstown and many places in between, as well as private residences, such as "Glen Osborne", Burnie, which has an ornate two-storey verandah with cast iron brackets, a valance, frieze and balustrade, and a colonial accommodation house, "Tahara", at Deloraine.

Hobart and Launceston both have excellent examples of ironwork fences and gateways. The entrance to the Royal Tasmanian Botanical Gardens consists of three hollow-capped posts supporting double vehicular gates and a single pedestrian gate, while a fence at the Launceston Showgrounds has ornamental cast iron bars, pointed caps and four-sided posts forming the cast iron railing. Cast iron drinking fountains, once common in city streets, are still found occasionally in parks.

Towns such as Richmond, Stanley, Longford, Evandale and the main midland bases are particularly notable for their wealth of 19th and early 20th century public and private buildings. The historic character of Kempton, Oatlands, Tunbridge and Ross has been further enhanced following the re-routing of the Midland Highway, which now by-passes the townships.

Richmond and Evandale, which are only a short distance from Hobart and Launceston, respectively, have become popular residential areas for people commuting to city workplaces, as well as prime destinations for visitors. Among Richmond's main structures are its bridge, the former gaol, St John's Church and St Luke's Church, the Old Granary, municipal buildings and others associated with the days when this was an important military post and convict station.

Richmond was on the main route between Hobart and the east coast and Port Arthur until the Sorell causeway was established in 1872. The convict-built Richmond Bridge, erected in 1823 over the Coal River, is the oldest surviving bridge in Australia. In the 1830s Richmond was Tasmania's third biggest town, earning itself the title "The Granary of Van Diemen's Land" as a result of its prolific production of wheat from wind, water and steam-driven mills. A simple miller's cottage, which has been restored, contrasts with the solid stone gaol that used to house convict road gangs engaged in public works, plus local law-breakers. In addition to the gaol, with its solitary cells, a cookhouse, women's ward and exercise yards, there is the former gaoler's residence. Dating back to 1825, the complex is one of Tasmania's earliest penal institutions.

Australia's oldest Roman Catholic church stands on a slight rise across the river from the town centre. St John's, a Gothic Revival church, was built in stages, the first one being completed in 1836. Its Gothic Revival appearance was largely due to the additions and reconstruction by the ex-convict architect Frederick Hugh Thomas in 1858 and 1859. Some of the interior timber was cut by convicts on the Tasman Peninsula. The Anglican

▲
Richmond: Bridge Street shops and one of the township's many Georgian cottages

church of St Luke's is also noteworthy. A focal point of this Georgian building, designed by John Lee Archer, is its clock tower and a clock that came from St David's, Hobart.

A granary is among the centres of commerce that have been recycled, especially in Bridge Street, to present new products whilst still retaining a feel for the past.

The same situation applies in Evandale, where antiques are sold from a former saddler's shop, breads and cakes are baked and sold in the one-time municipal offices, a restaurant operates in an old butchery and the stables of the former Royal Oak Hotel have been transformed into an art gallery.

Founded in 1816, Evandale is an important agricultural and administrative centre. A dominant feature is its water tower, one of two erected at the end of last century. It is similar in style to those established early in the 19th century on the British coastline. A hydraulic turbine pumped water from a plant five kilometres away, but the plant was destroyed during massive floods that swept through the area in 1929. Inns of the past and present, churches and classic Georgian shops and residences contribute to Evandale's village atmosphere.

The Bishop's chair in St Andrew's Church of England was made from the oak timbers of Australia's first warship, HMS Nelson, while history that is closer to home is depicted in the 1847 Clarendon Arms Hotel, where murals highlight key aspects of settlement and exploration in northern Tasmania.

This area is closely associated with the voyage that led to the founding of Melbourne in 1835 as one of the leaders of the expedition, John Batman, lived at nearby "Kingston", a property established in 1822. A three-room stone cottage, a lock-up and brick storeroom were restored during the 1950s and the contents of the cottage include the original deed of grant, which hangs over a fireplace.

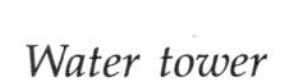

Evandale (clockwise):

Water tower

"Blenheim", established in 1832 as the Patriot King William IV Inn, is now a craft outlet

St Andrew's Uniting Church, dating back to 1840

Evandale Library, founded in 1847, is one of Australia's oldest country libraries

Quaint stores in Russell Street

Evandale Post Office - classic Victorian architecture

A D

Attention to detail is abundant on small country buildings as well as grand establishments, as evidenced in this outbuilding near Kempton and "Mona Vale", in the Ross district. "Mona Vale" is an outstanding Italianate villa that is sometimes referred to as the "Calendar House" as it has 365 windows, 7 entrances, 52 rooms and 12 chimneys. The third house on the property, it was built between 1865 and 1869 for Robert Kermode. "Mona Vale" is not open to the public
(By permission of Mr and Mrs E.A. Cameron)

Longford:

Christ Church (above)

(Right clockwise) Municipal Hall and environs

Wellington Street by night

Interesting outbuildings at "Woolmers" include the coachhouse, now colonial accommodation (By permission of Thomas Archer)

Stuccoed pilasters flank entrances to the Longford Library, formerly the Tattersall's Hotel

Racecourse Hotel

Many of the early settlers of Evandale, Longford and New Norfolk came from Norfolk Island, with the Longford area initially being called Norfolk Plains. The newcomers imported acorns, willow slips, hawthorn and briar berries and poplar seeds so they could recreate the atmosphere of the English homeland they had left some years beforehand. The fruits of their labour can still be seen in the hawthorns lining roadsides near Longford and the large stands of deciduous English trees.

One of Longford's most interesting buildings is Christ Church, erected by convicts in 1839 and featuring stained glass windows and a tower with a clock provided by the Government. The west window, designed by William Archer, of "Cheshunt", Deloraine, was presented by a resident, Charles Reid. It cost £300 and is regarded as one of the finest church windows in Australia.

Mills have played an important role here, especially during the period early last century when this was a major wheat-growing area for the settlements at Port Jackson and Port Phillip. The old Ritchie's Mill near the village green and the four-storey mill once operated by Thomas Affleck in Union Street have been recycled but others are now in ruins.

The earliest public building, the toll house in Wellington Street, is a simple 1835 structure with an unusual central chimney with recessed panels. The Racecourse Hotel, which is now part of Tasmania's colonial accommodation network, has also stood the test of time. It features two front entrances - a four-panelled door and a pair of half-glazed doors with transom lights - and four dormers.

A number of other old inns have been converted into private residences, adding to the list of eminent country houses in the surrounding district. These include the properties of the pioneering Archer family: "Woolmers" (Thomas Archer, 1819) "Brickendon", built in 1831 by William Archer, "Panshanger" (Joseph Archer, 1831) and "Northbury" (Edward Archer, 1862). The Classical front of "Woolmers" was added in 1831 to the original brick-nogged weatherboard section, which is now at the rear. Thomas Archer's son, William, was an accomplished architect but he generally restricted his talents to the designing of family homes or those of close relatives, including William Kermode, his brother-in-law, who established the present "Mona Vale" near Ross.

New Norfolk, formerly called Elizabeth Town, was first settled by Europeans in 1808. Over the years it became an important centre for the hop industry and it is still a service centre for other rural and manufacturing industries.

Among New Norfolk's notable buildings is St Matthew's Church, which incorporates the walls and floor of the nave of Tasmania's oldest church, erected in 1823. Together with the adjoining Gothic Revival hall and a two-storey rectory, this is an important group of buildings in the town centre.

The Bush Inn has been part of the New Norfolk scene since 1825, with a number of additions to the hostelry since then. This is a community meeting place, with even the local Methodists holding their first gathering in the pub.

RACECOURSE HOTEL

Kodak
PHOTO PROCESSING
AVAILABLE HERE

CARLTON DRAUGHT

The River Derwent is crossed here by a modern bridge that replaced three earlier ones, including the original link funded by private enterprise and built with logs shaped from gum trees. A toll was charged for use of the bridge to help offset the construction costs, and the quaint octagonal tollhouse built in 1841 is still in service - as a youth hostel!

Tasmania has many historic bridges as well as graceful modern structures, such as the the Tasman Bridge, which crosses the Derwent farther downstream at Hobart. Dating from 1964, it replaced a floating pontoon bridge that had been synonymous with Hobart for the preceding 20 years. The Tasman Bridge was a focus of attention in 1975 when a large section collapsed after the structure was hit by a bulk ore carrier. It was a further two years before the main link between Hobart's eastern and western shores was restored, a period that was marked by substantial economic and social unheaval in the city.

Hobart's other bridges include another technologically interesting one, albeit a much smaller 1ink. It is the counterweighted drawbridge adjoining Constitution Dock - the only structure of this type in Australia. Built in the 1930s and raised by a low-powered electric motor, it was designed to provide rail access to the Elizabeth Street pier. Extensive restoration work in 1990 has ensured its preservation.

In the North, the Batman Bridge, which spans the Tamar River at Whirlpool Reach, joined the ranks of the early cable-stayed truss bridges when it was opened in 1968. A 96-metre-high A-frame supports the structure through giant, concrete-filled steel cables that are anchored to bedrock 21 metres underground. One of the most unusual bridges, however, is the Spiky Bridge near Swansea. This massive, flat-topped structure was built between 1845 and 1848 by convicts, presumably from the Rocky Hills probation station. Fieldstones are the main material, the jagged surface of the parapet resulting from the vertical and uneven placement of stones.

In Swansea, itself, freestone, bluestone and drystone are used in many buildings and walls. Morris' General Store stands like a sentinel on the spot it has occupied since it was built for Mr J.A. Graham as a single-storey store in 1845. Ten years later, two more floors were added to the Georgian stone building, which was run by the Morris family for more than a century.

Industry of another kind went into operating a bark mill that opened in the 1890s. During the Depression the mill provided income for locals, who received about sixpence for a bundle of black wattle bark that was subsequently used for tanning heavy leathers. Materials utilised during restoration of the mill in the 1980s included the original Oyster Bay pine posts and rafters.

There are also a number of interesting buildings south of Swansea. Of particular note are picturesque "Mitchell Cottage", once a church and schoolhouse

▲▲▲
Tollhouse, New Norfolk, now a youth hostel
▲▲
Morris' General Store, Swansea, complete with a ring for tethering horses!

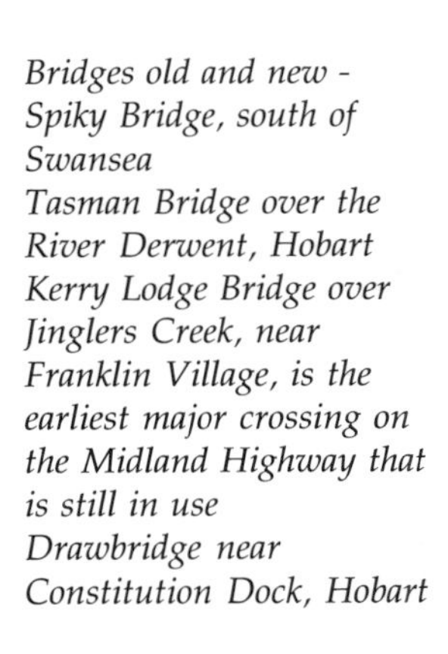

Bridges old and new -
Spiky Bridge, south of Swansea
Tasman Bridge over the River Derwent, Hobart
Kerry Lodge Bridge over Jinglers Creek, near Franklin Village, is the earliest major crossing on the Midland Highway that is still in use
Drawbridge near Constitution Dock, Hobart

▲
Fieldstone conjoined workers' cottages, "Mayfield"

▶
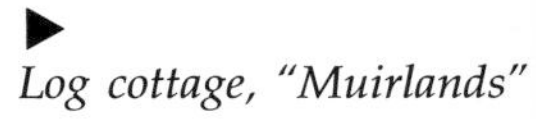
Log cottage, "Muirlands"

Main street, Queenstown

for one of the district's largest properties, "Lisdillon", the homestead and outbuildings of the adjoining estate, "Mayfield", and a log barn and former blacksmith's shop at "Muirlands". "Mitchell Cottage" is constructed from random rubble bound with burnt seashell, while stone, brick and fieldstone have been used in the "Mayfield" structures. It is relatively unusual to find log buildings that have survived as well as the log barn and cottage at "Muirlands". Together with a yard surround of chock and log fencing, they illustrate a rare building pattern.

In another instance, low stone walls that are the only remains of a long-gone saltworks' bakehouse have been incorporated in a new complex at Great Oyster Bay. The walls are capped with galvanised iron and form part of the living area of the house.

In the 1830s, there were saltworks at "Lisdillon" and near Woodbury, in the Midlands, where two salt pans gave rise to the name "Salt Pan Plains." The following description of the midland pans is from Ross' Almanack of 1830:

"In Winter they are filled with rainwater, which is dried up in Summer, when they become covered with a crust of excellent salt, fit for any culinary purpose, presenting a surface as white as snow, from a quarter to about half an inch thick. Several tons are collected annually from the neighbourhood."

Meanwhile, across the island on the west coast, fortunes were to be made from extraction of another kind - mining. The main towns that sprang up to service the industry were Queenstown and Zeehan, with Strahan continuing its role as a key port. Queenstown's buildings nestling between the steep surrounding hills include the Empire Hotel, which once boasted having "hot and cold baths and a day and night porter." This hotel is a legacy of the boom times at the turn of the century when the town had 14 hotels servicing its 5,000 residents. Then, as now, the manager of the Mount Lyell Company, which operates Queenstown's mines, lived in "Penghana", an 1895 brick house set amidst extensive gardens on a hill overlooking the town.

Many of the buildings in Strahan, to the south, and Zeehan, to the north, date from the same period, but Zeehan also has a number of "older veterans." During its heyday towards the end of last century the town had the largest Stock Exchange in Australia, with members from as far afield as New Zealand. At the same time, the Gaiety Theatre was alive with star performers of the calibre of Dame Nellie Melba and a prestigous School of Mines was established in a building that now houses the West Coast Pioneers' Memorial Museum. The theatre has survived but the Stock Exchange has long since gone!

POST ZEEHAN OFFICE

ZEEHAN

▲▲
Stanley streetscape and old bond store

◀
Zeehan, looking towards Post Office (with detail) and Gaiety Theatre

◀
Regatta Point and detail of railway station, once an important West Coast base

Stanley, in the North-West, is one of Tasmania's best-preserved historic towns. The streets winding round the base of The Nut, a 120-metre-high basalt formation at Circular Head, are filled with cottages, hotels, stores and other commercial buildings of the 19th and early 20th centuries.

Bluestone quarried from The Nut was used to build a dry-laid retaining wall that divides Alexander Terrace leading to the waterfront. Near the wharf is a stone building that was formerly a grain store, the construction materials having arrived in Stanley as ships' ballast. The old Van Diemen's Land Company store, which is also on the waterfront, has had a variety of purposes over the years: a store, a base for holding convicts, a customs house, a dairy factory and a fish processing factory. Ownership is now vested with the State Government.

The Van Diemen's Land Company was responsible for the development of Stanley, the first major north-western settlement. Architect John Lee Archer, who was assigned the task of designing the township, which serviced the nearby "Highfield Estate" and the company's property, "Woolnorth", is buried in Stanley's cemetery.

Regency-style "Highfield", the home of the company's Chief Agent until 1856, was purchased by the Tasmanian Government in 1982, with funding assistance from the National Estate. The house and outbuildings, including bluestone stables that contain displays of memorabilia from "Highfield" and "Woolnorth", a chapel, threshing barns, a cart shed and cottages are now the subject of extensive preservation and restoration.

Many north-western buildings are made of local timber. Machine-sawn hardwoods were readily available late in the 19th century and construction was undertaken by local carpenters. Shingle-roofed St Stephen's Church of England, Penguin, is an enduring example.

Westbury is another town in the North-West that retains many of its old buildings, including The White House, erected by the village green in the 1840s as Thomas White's Token Store, and Fitzpatrick's Inn, which began operations in 1833. This former inn is Georgian in style but has a Classical portico and Tuscan columns that were added in the early 1900s. Fitzpatrick's Inn and St Andrew's Church are among the landmarks of Westbury, the church being noted, in particular, for its carvings by the late Mrs Nellie Payne, who lived in the district.

Another significant church, St Mark's Church of England, "keeps watch" on the township of Deloraine from its hilltop site. The 1859 brick Gothic Revival building, designed by W.H. Clayton, one of the first Australian-born architects of the 19th century, features an elegant three-level tower and spire.

Old inns and mills, such as the Bowerbank Mill, which is said to have had a gold sovereign embedded in its chimney during construction, are key elements of the landscape in Deloraine, an important agricultural centre since the 1840s.

A two-storey former warehouse built of bluestone in Parsonage Street and the Baptist Tabernacle are among other buildings on the Register of the National Estate.

Perth, 18 kilometres south of Launceston, also has a distinctive Baptist Tabernacle. The octagonal 1889 building has a high domed iron roof and its architectural interest extends to the panelled doors and half-round transom light at the entrance, which are capped with a moulded surround.

All of Tasmania's midland towns have historic connections, often resulting from their establishment as military posts (Ross, Oatlands, Bothwell and Campbell Town). They were also strategically located for stage coach changes, hence their propensity of inns. The main role of these

33

◀
Georgian styling in a Deloraine shop and residence, which was formerly a hospital, and in Fitzpatrick's Inn, Deloraine

▲
A drinking fountain for horses is a feature in the grounds of Fitzpatrick's Inn

centres nowadays, however, is to service the surrounding rural areas.

Like Ross and Richmond, Campbell Town also has an arched bridge built by convicts, but this one is made of bricks rather than stone. It is over the Elizabeth River, which Governor Macquarie named after his wife. The township, itself, also derives its name from Mrs Macquarie, who had been Elizabeth Henrietta Campbell. The outstanding buildings of this township include St John's Presbyterian Church, which contains an organ and desk that belonged to the first Anglican Bishop of Tasmania, Bishop Nixon, a former inn, the Foxhunter's Return, an old brewery and the Campbell Town Inn. The outside walls and stone stables of the rubble stone Foxhunter's Return, which has a main facade of rusticated ashlar, form a courtyard, while the brewery, built in 1840 by publican Hugh Kean and later occupied by the Masonic Lodge, has an ashlar face of six bays. The rather forlorn brewery typifies industrial buildings that are now obsolete. The Campbell Town Inn, built by Hugh Kean in 1840 for Gavin Hogg, has a staircase carved from solid sandstone.

In King Street, the simple Wesleyan Chapel has taken on a new lease of life following its restoration by the Midlands Group of the National Trust and conversion into a community meeting and display centre. This is the second chapel on the site, bricks from the first one, which dated back to 1838, having been incorporated in an outbuilding. The cedar-lined chapel was used as a Sunday School for many years after the congregation outgrew the tiny building.

The township of Ross also has many reminders of the past and, in particular, the endeavours of the convicts and other craftsmen of varied eras who built the many English-style stone cottages, the Municipal Council Chambers (originally the Police Court), the old Ordnance Office, with the ordnance coat-of-arms and 1836 date worked into the stone, and the impressive war memorial. The Old Barracks, restored by the National Trust, are near the town centre with its four corners said to represent temptation (a hotel), recreation (the Town Hall), salvation (a church) and damnation (the old gaol).

The Man O'Ross Hotel is another old-timer. Built in 1831, it has a number of mileposts in the grounds. Refreshments are also offered at the Scotch Thistle Inn - although the customers are somewhat different from those of the past when this was the local midwifery centre!

Mellowed churches add to the atmosphere of Ross but its most significant attraction is its arched freestone bridge with the remarkable carvings of Daniel Herbert (discussed in the section on Convicts and their Contribution). This bridge replaced an earlier timber structure up-river that had become impassable by 1831. The construction work finally began in 1833, the bridge being designed by John Lee Archer, who allegedly had trouble dealing with other people involved in the project. So much so that one local resident commented during

▲▲▲ *Victorian bluestone warehouse in Parsonage Street, Deloraine*

▲▲ *Foxhunter's Return, Campbell Town*

▲ *The Masonic Lodge, Campbell Town, was built as a brewery*

▲ *Ross Post Office, complete with old-style telephone box*

◀ *Man O' Ross Hotel*

◀▼ *Stone and timber combined in a Ross dwelling*

the course of construction that "our bridge will bridge nothing but a gap in the conversation." He was proved wrong, however, as this is now Australia's third oldest bridge and is regarded as the most important from an architectural point of view.

Stone, the predominant building material in Ross, was also used for the Tasmanian Wool Centre, which opened in 1988. Lined with Tasmanian timber, this centre has a crafts section, a museum and exhibitions that outline the history of Australian wool production and, in particular, the importance of the contribution of woolgrowers and others associated with the industry in Ross and elsewhere in Tasmania's Midlands.

Some of the State's finest country homes are found in the Ross district. They include "Beaufront", a single-storey Georgian stone house with a Regency bow on the west facade, which was built in 1837, "Mona Vale", built between 1865 and 1869 for Robert Kermode, and "Ellinthorpe", which was famous as a 19th century girls' college. Run by Mrs George Carr Clark, whose husband owned the property, the college was regarded in 1830 as the best girls' school in Australia.

The ruins of another college that is important in Tasmania's education history, Horton College, are just south of Ross near the Midland Highway.

◀
Municipal offices and war memorial, Ross

▼▼
Rustic fences contribute to Oatlands' character

▼
Locally quarried sandstone is used extensively in buildings and surrounds

▲
Cantwell's Shop, Oatlands

Built in the mid-19th century by Captain Samuel Horton, the boys' college closed in 1892 and was demolished 28 years later.

Oatlands was visited in 1821 by Governor Macquarie, who described it as "a very eligible situation for a town." Most of Oatlands' buildings were erected in the first half of the 19th century, often from locally quarried sandstone, which was also used for outbuildings, walls and pavements. Nowadays, the buildings display the largest collection of Georgian architectural styles in any one centre in Australia. In the boom days of the 1830s life revolved around military operations and local industries such as brewing and milling. Among the associated buildings that still remain are the Supreme Court House, which was established in 1829 and has been restored by the National Trust, an 1835 gaoler's residence and the Callington Mill complex, complete with a miller's cottage. Other substantial buildings include old churches and inns, "Holyrood House", which was built in 1840 for police magistrate John Whitefoord, and has also served as a school and a restaurant, and the 1881 Victorian-style Town Hall, which occupies a dominant position in the main street.

Several properties have been recycled to provide visitor accommodation but, basically, the streetscapes of Oatlands have remained much the same for over a century.

Inns were also prevalent in Kempton when this, too, was a stage coach stop. Additional custom came from townspeople involved in brewing, milling, tanning, blacksmithing, shoemaking and carpentry, all of which were well-established in the Green Ponds area by 1829. The Wilmot Arms Inn, a Georgian coaching house, is among the survivors.

Kempton, named after the Kemp family, who were early settlers, flourished during the days of roadbuilding between Hobart and Launceston. It was also the first marketplace in Tasmania for stock and produce.

The sandstone church of St Mary's, completed in 1844, has the original alms box, which was used to collect offerings for distribution to the poor of the parish. The church, with its truncated tower and timber belfry, is believed to have been designed by James Blackburn.

Today, Kempton's buildings reflect both the utilitarian and the refined aspects of its 19th century development.

Inland, the township of Bothwell has a distinctive Tasmanian Georgian character. Scottish settlers were among those who came here in the 1820s and links with that country are still evident through events like the annual Highland Spin-In, which attracts hundreds of spinners and weavers who produce knitted squares from Bothwell's famed wool.

Avenue plantings of trees enhance the town's many sandstone and convict brick dwellings and commercial properties, its timber cottages and mellowed churches. St Lukes Church, completed

▲▲▲ *Memorial erected in Kempton after World War 1*

▲▲ *"Fernleigh", Kempton*

▲ *Kempton store*

in 1831, is the oldest Presbyterian church in Australia, and for the first 60 years it was used by both Presbyterian and Anglican churchgoers. It is another of architect John Lee Archer's designs, with special attention centred on the square Norman tower and the clock. St Luke's was extensively restored during the 1980s.

Anglicans obtained their own church in 1891 when St Michael and All Angels was built. It is made of local stone, which is also featured in solid seats in the porch and in a circular staircase leading to the belfry. St Michael's is by Queens Square, where there is a sundial that is believed to be the only four-faced vertical one in the southern hemisphere. It is a memorial to people from the district who died in World War 1.

The Post Office, built in 1891 for the Van Diemen's Land Bank, still has the original hitching rail at the front, while the Castle Hotel, which first appeared on licensing records in 1829, contains photographs and other mementoes of "the good old days."

Private residences of note include an 1850 two-storey brick and stuccoed building in Dalrymple Street referred to as the "Coffee Palace". Its uses have included a hotel and a doctor's surgery. Across the Clyde River is "Wentworth House", built in 1833 by Bothwell magistrate Captain D'Arcy Wentworth, whose brother achieved fame for his crossing of the Blue Mountains in New South Wales. "Fort Wentworth", with the date 1832 inscribed above the central doorway, has the names of prisoners, dates and sketches of sailing ships scratched into cell walls. This ashlar stone fort, which later became a police office and watchhouse, is now privately owned.

A number of buildings in Hamilton, another classified historic town in the central region, have been recycled to cater for tourism activities. Imposing "Glen Clyde House", once an inn, is now an art and craft centre, while single-storey Georgian sandstone cottages, a former schoolhouse and several nearby farms have been opened up for visitor accommodation. St Peter's Church, completed in 1836, is among the oldest buildings.

In terms of Tasmania's new towns, the 20th century has been marked by the development of small settlements based on hydro projects - Tarraleah, Waddamana, Miena, Poatina and Strathgordan - and mining activities, involving places such as Luina. However, ghost towns like Boobyalla, Lefroy, Linda, Gormanston and Pillinger are gradually being joined by some of these as they wind down in response to changes in mining and hydro operations. This pattern is likely to continue as improved transport and communication systems make it easier for workers at remote sites, such as the Hellyer Mine 80 kilometres south of Burnie, to commute from large residential centres to their places of employment and for companies and organisations to operate in isolated areas.

▲
St Luke's Church, Bothwell, with carvings attributed to Daniel Herbert

Victoria's Cottage, Hamilton, part of the colonial accommodation network

Bothwell Post Office, formerly the Van Diemen's Land Bank

Bothwell stores

Industry and Commerce

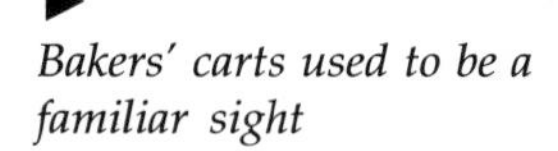

◀
Gretna in the Derwent Valley

▶
Bakers' carts used to be a familiar sight

In the first half of the 19th century Tasmania's economy was based on rural and whaling activities. This was followed by the mining era, the exploitation of water for the generation of electricity and the development of a modern industrial State based on forestry, mining, agriculture, fishing, manufacturing and tourism.

A prime aim at the time of European settlement was to ensure that there was adequate food for the colony. Agricultural pursuits centred on the production of grain, sheep and cattle, and, later, fruit.

In 1810 the *Venus* arrived from Calcutta with fresh, uncontaminated seed that laid the foundation for agriculture and helped to alleviate famine. Cereals were imported from India because floods in the Hawkesbury region of New South Wales had resulted in extremely high prices for maize and wheat.

It wasn't long before Tasmania reversed its position and became an exporter, rather than an importer, with wheat among the first commodities to be sent to the neighbouring colony.

These days, barley is the most important cereal grain crop, followed by oats and wheat. The North-West has the largest area devoted to sown pastures and it produces nearly half the State's hay.

Restored, derelict or ruined mills throughout the island reflect the endeavours of pioneers and others who followed in their footsteps. The Callington Mill at Oatlands was among those driven by wind but most mills established before the days of steam and electric power were water-driven.

Restored ones include the Thorpe Mill at Bothwell, which Thomas Axford built for flour milling soon after he reached the district in 1822. It is one of the few operational water-powered mills in Australia.

Development of the Penny Royal complex in Launceston in the 1970s has enabled thousands of people to gain a better understanding of the mechanics and methods of early watermills and cornmills. Launceston's restored 1840 watermill and 1825 cornmill originally stood at "Barton", near Cressy, where they were built by Andrew Gatenby and his four sons after their arrival from England in 1823.

Farmers took their grain from as far away as the Fingal Valley to be ground into flour at the "Barton" mill. However, new milling methods towards the end of last century resulted in a decline in customers and this, coupled with repeated flooding, led to the abandonment of the mill. After being dismantled in 1972 it was moved

▲
Thorpe Mill, Bothwell

▲▲
Workings, Thorpe Mill

▲
Monds Mill, Carrick

◀◀
Callington Mill, Oatlands

◀
Miller's cottage, Callington Mill

▲ *"Macquarie House", Launceston*

stone by stone to its present location.

A number of mills have been recycled, the Bowerbank Mill at Deloraine becoming an art gallery for many years and the four-level bluestone Monds mill at Carrick, complete with a miller's cottage, having also served as a restaurant.

Launceston has a number of "revived" mills including Ritchies Mill, now an art centre. Milling continued here until 1973 - a period of nearly 140 years. The adjoining silos are topped by an unusual wooden structure, while a two-storey Georgian mill cottage, dating back to 1835, completes the complex.

Although not directly associated with milling, another Launceston building, "Macquarie House", also has links with grain-growing. It was built in 1830 as a warehouse for merchant Henry Reed, who supplied provisions for the expedition from Launceston to Victoria by John Batman and John Pascoe Fawkner. Grain was among the goods stored in "Macquarie House", which is now an annexe of the Queen Victoria Museum and Art Gallery and features displays of photographs and items associated with Launceston in its early days. Standing in Civic Square, it provides a striking contrast to the modern commercial buildings of the surrounding area.

Wool was grown from 1806, Merinos having been brought from Port Jackson, but the first imports of significance didn't arrive until 1820. They came from two main sources: Sheep imported from the Spanish flock of King George 111 in England and others from Saxony, where Spanish Merinos had thrived for some time.

The export of Tasmanian wool began in 1822, Hobart merchant and philanthropist Henry Hopkins taking 12 bales of wool to London in his vessel, the *Nautilus*. The wool was bought in Tasmania for fourpence per pound and sold in London for sevenpence.

A number of settlers who reached Tasmania in the 1820s became pioneers of the wool and fat lamb industries, with many of their descendants still farming the same land today. The first ship to sail direct from England to Hobart Town on private charter, the *Emerald*, arrived in 1821. Her passengers included Adam and John Amos and their families, who settled at Cranbrook, just north of Swansea, and another east coast pioneer, George Meredith, whose daughter-in-law, Louisa Anne Meredith, became the well-known author and artist.

Rural scene in vicinity of St Patrick's Head Pinnacle, near St Marys

The Van Diemen's Land Company established "Highfield" in the North-West

▶▶
View to Stanley from "Highfield"

▶▶
Friesian cattle

A tablet behind the pulpit of the Gala Kirk, which was erected at Cranbrook in 1845, was installed on the 100th anniversary of the Amos' landing.

Thomas Archer, who came from Hertford, England, was the first of four brothers who developed properties, notably in the Longford district, that are still among the island's foremost rural estates.

In 1824, Roderic O'Connor arrived from Dublin in his own ship, the *Ardent*, bringing with him farming implements, waggons, carts, a large town clock and a bell! "Connorville", near Cressy, one of the State's showpieces, is still owned by the O'Connor family. In 1989, a 100-kilogram bale of superfine merino wool from "Connorville" was bought by the Japanese firm, Fujii Keori, a consistent high bidder for Tasmania's superfine wool, for a price of 300,850 cents per kilo - ten times more than the previous record.

Bothwell and the Derwent Valley are among other areas with properties that have been worked by successive generations of settler families.

In the 1830 Ross' Almanack, praise was bestowed on two Fingal Valley pioneers, James Grant, of "Tullochgorum", and the Hon. William Talbot, of "Malahide", for their efforts in agricultural development...

"We cannot refrain from mentioning here, the laudable exertions of both Mr James Grant and Mr Talbot in the improvement of wool, each sending large quantities annually of their own growth to the London market, of such a quality as to command very remunerating, and not withstanding the late depression, increasing prices."

Another insertion went on to say that *"It has of late become fashionable in London, and especially in Edinburgh, for ladies to wear evening shawls of Van Diemen's Land wool of the finer qualities, as having a singular softness, and imparting a comfort to the back and shoulders peculiarly its own."*

The Van Diemen's Land Company was among other significant contributors to the improvement of sheep stocks on its own holdings in the North-West and on those of midland sheep breeders whom it supplied with Merinos imported from Saxony and England. A number of private landowners in various parts of Tasmania also imported stocks from these sources.

Nowadays, the island is famous for its superfine merino wool and for the work undertaken here in relation to the development of the Australasian sheep breeds Polwarth and Corriedale. The earliest Tasmanian Corriedale stud was established at "Mountford", Longford, in 1881, and Polwarths were introduced to the State from Victoria at the beginning of this century. A more recent addition, Cormos, were bred originally at "Dungrove", Bothwell. They were specifically developed to suit local conditions and to provide a highly fertile breed with a good wool yield.

The history of manufacturing companies like

Coats Paton (Australia) Limited, which produces woollen products in Launceston, the Waverley Woollen Mills, established in Launceston in 1874, and the Tamar Knitting Mills, Launceston, are inextricably linked with the heritage of Tasmanian sheep and fine wool production.

The first cattle, which were brought to the island in 1807, resembled coarse bullocks, but these were soon supplemented with superior animals from England. A herd of Aberdeen Angus cattle introduced at Bothwell in 1822 by Captain Patrick Wood, who settled at "Dennistoun", is believed to be Australia's oldest pedigree herd. The nation's first Hereford herd was owned by the Van Diemen's Land Company, which at one stage also had Australia's foremost Shorthorn herd.

Melville's Van Diemen's Land Annual of 1834 stated that *"at present, either for the yoke or the pail, for docility or for hardiness, the improved breed of cattle, which is rapidly taking place of all others, cannot be surpassed, either in England or other parts of the world."*

Shortly before, a report extolling the virtues of Campbell Town claimed *"the natural herbage is so rich, with its character for producing fat cattle so well established that the butchers of Hobart town come to it to purchase a large proportion of their meat, although the nearest part of it is 70 miles distant."*

Much of the island's breeding stock in the 1820s came from stockmarkets at Cross Marsh (Kempton) and Ross, where there was a government stockyard.

Today, the main cattle breeds for milk production are Friesians, Jerseys and Ayrshires, with a smaller number of milking Shorthorns and Guernseys. The traditional beef cattle - Herefords, Aberdeen Angus, Shorthorns and Devons - have been joined by the newer lines of Brahmans, Murray Greys and Charolais.

Tasmania's dairy herds, notably in the North-West and on King Island, supply the milk that is used for the production of the State's internationally acclaimed dairy products. Of particular note are the cheeses, butter and creams from the factories of United Milk Tasmania Limited, Lactos Proprietary Limited and the King Island Dairy, which have contributed to Tasmania's recently earned reputation as a "gourmand's paradise."

For decades, cocoa and chocolate manufacturer Cadbury Schweppes Proprietary Limited (formerly Cadbury-Fry Pascall) has promoted the use of local milk in its confectionary. This extensive plant at Claremont began operating in 1920 but was hit by the Depression and did not function independently of its parent company in England until the 1930s. Cadbury "by mountain and sea" has played an important part in the development of industry and the community, in general.

Barn at "Hilly Park", in the Oatlands district, and a sheep dip on the property that dates back to the 1830s

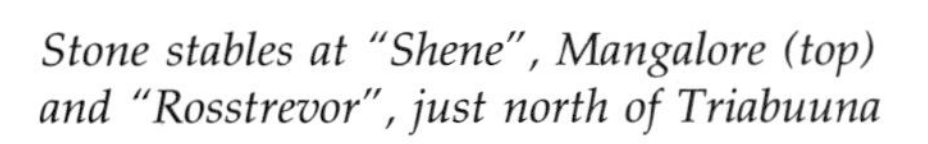

Stone stables at "Shene", Mangalore (top) and "Rosstrevor", just north of Triabuuna

▲▲▲ *Stables at "Highfield"*

▲▲ *Log barn and former blacksmith's shop, "Muirlands", east coast*

▲ *Furphy water cart, Tunbridge, of the type used extensively from the late 19th century, especially during World War 1*

Last century, many farmers, especially in the Midlands, bred racehorses on pedigree lines and often had their own private training courses. The original horses, strong Arab crosses, were brought from New South Wales but, as with sheep and cattle, the lines were steadily improved. Horses bred and trained in Tasmania are among the winners of Australia's most prestigious horse race, the Melbourne Cup.

Picnic race meetings were a feature of early social life in the colony. The first race meeting took place in a paddock at New Town in 1814, but other courses were established before long at Sandy Bay Beach, by the New Town Rivulet and in a number of country centres, including Jericho, Ross and Longford. Not everyone was convinced, however, that the races were in the best interests of the community. In 1831 it was reported that *"although races are conducted with much propriety, and no drinking, low gambling or riot is permitted at them, it is a question whether the benefit they may confer on the colony as a spur to the improvement of the horse, especially of that breed which it is expected will ultimately become a profitable export to India, and the innocent, are not more than counterbalanced by the injury and encroachment it occasions to the habits of the labouring classes in a community so peculiarly constituted as ours. The former inveterate habits, and the almost invincible inclination to drinking and dissipation in the convict population, necessary to be kept down at all times by a certain restraint, break out at such times like a species of wildfire, which it often requires many days to quench."*

Among the early clubs was the Tasmanian Racing Club, which was formed in 1874 and still uses its original starting bell. The Tasmanian Racing Authority, which is part of the Department of Tourism, Sport and Recreation, is now the "umbrella" body for Tasmanian horseracing.

For many years Tasmania has been called the Apple Isle, relating to its pre-eminence in the first half of this century as an apple producing and exporting land. Its potential for orcharding was recognised well before this, however. Referring to the inferior quality of early fruit such as apples and peaches, it was declared in 1830 that *"the soil and climate of Van Diemen's Land give it so decidely the character of a cider country, that for some time past a growing taste has prevailed to introduce better kinds, and to improve the quality of the fruit."*

The climate had also proved favourable for growing pears, raspberries, strawberries, currants, cherries and plums - all of which are still produced commercially.

A trial shipment of 100 cases of apples was sent to England in 1884 but earlier exports had gone to neighbouring colonies, New Zealand, Rio de Janeiro and Cape Town. In 1887, 4,000 cases were taken by the Orient Steam Navigation Company to Melbourne, from where they were trans-shipped to England.

Growers formed a co-operative and contracted the Anglo-Australian Steamship Company (the Port Line) to call at Tasmania before sailing directly overseas. In the heyday of fruit exporting,the wharves of Hobart, Port Huon and Beauty Point were lined with ships taking on cargo. The Huon and Tamar Valleys were the main apple and pear-growing areas, while berry and small-fruit growing were concentrated in the Derwent and Huon Valleys.

Rationalisation of the apple and pear industries during the 1960s resulted in the grubbing of many trees. The European export market has now declined but about 20% of the apple crop is still sold overseas, primarily in Asia.

The heritage of Tasmania's apple industry is preserved in a museum at Grove, where the display items include hundreds of different Tasmanian apple case labels and an apple grader developed late last century by Joseph Lomas, of Huonville.

The processing of small fruits into jams and preserves was an extremely important part of the fruit industry for about 70 years from the latter part of the 19th century. The most famous establishment was that of Henry Jones, who was knighted in 1919 for "good and faithful services to Ourselves and the Empire."

The nine connected former warehouses at the Old Wharf, Hobart, are still often referred to as the "Jones and Co. buildings". At one stage they contained the largest, best-equipped and most modern jam factory in the southern hemisphere. There was a tin-making plant, fruit canning works and a cool storage plant, which housed fruit, hops, meat, fish, butter and eggs and, in addition, manufactured most of southern Tasmania's ice requirements. It had been a jam and fruit preserving factory for some time before Henry Jones began work there for George Peacock in 1874, at the age of 12 years. Henry rose through the ranks from a label-paster to the leader of one of Tasmania's most successful industrial empires.

When asked why he chose the name IXL for the jams and processed fruits he produced, Sir Henry replied, "I Excell in all the products I make. It is my motto."

As the business expanded other factories became associated with the Hobart operation, the Henry Jones Co-operative Limited being formed to control its interests in Tasmania, on the Australian mainland and in South Africa. Jones and Co. continued to flourish long after Sir Henry's death in 1926, but eventually the IXL factory was closed and the business was transferred to Melbourne because of the economic advantage of having a mainland base at that time.

Jones and Co. was also involved in the hop industry and at one stage owned the largest hopfield in the southern hemisphere.

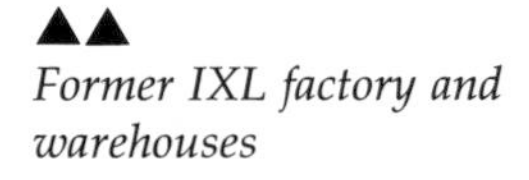

▲▲
Former IXL factory and warehouses

▲
Products of the "Apple Isle"

▶▶
Oast houses and hop kilns dot the Derwent Valley. The oast house (top) now houses a hop museum

Tasmania still produces approximately three-quarters of Australia's hops and it supplies both interstate and overseas markets.

Hops were grown in Tasmania as early as 1804 when Lieutenant-Colonel Paterson settled in the Tamar region. However, the acknowledged founder of the industry was William Shoobridge, who planted hops brought from England in Providence Valley (near Newedgate Street, North Hobart) in 1822. By the 1830s, hop cultivation had mainly moved to the New Norfolk district, with the area under hops in 1854 totalling 55 acres.

For generations, the hop-harvesting season was of paramount importance to Derwent Valley residents and those who travelled on special trains that ran from Hobart to Bushy Park to carry hop-pickers. Early this century, schools in the New Norfolk district closed for "hop holidays" so that children could join their families in the field work and thus boost incomes. The scene is now quite different, with the introduction of new high-yielding hop varieties resulting in the concentration of hopfields in large lots that are suitable for mechanical harvesting. Many of the hops are pelletised before being shipped to breweries around the world.

The main production areas these days are in the North-West and North-East and, to a lesser extent, at Bushy Park and Ranelagh in the Huon Valley.

Oast houses dotting the Derwent Valley indicate the extent of this industry in the past, with one of the buildings at New Norfolk housing a museum that outlines the history of hop-growing in Tasmania.

Local purchasers of hops include the Cascade Brewery Company, which operates Boags Brewery in Launceston and the Cascade Brewery, Hobart. They are remnants of a far greater network of breweries that once operated in Tasmania. Tooth's Brewery, for instance, was established in Hampden Road, Battery Point, by Edwin Tooth between 1847 and 1851. In 1873 it was converted into a hat factory by Mr Joseph Bidencope, the "father of the hat industry in Australia", and three years later Bidencope's hats and materials were shown in an exhibition in Philadelphia (USA). Some of Bidencope's display items are still held in Philadelphia's National Museum. The next stage of the former brewery's life was as a malt factory and, more recently, it has been professional offices.

The original Cascade brewery erected in 1832 at the base of Mount Wellington was rebuilt in 1927, when the top three storeys were added, and, again, after it was devastated by bushfires on Black Tuesday, 7 February 1967.

This is the oldest continuously operated manufacturing enterprise in Australia, the brewing operations far outliving the sawmilling and flour milling activities that were also carried on here from 1824 by Cascade founder, Peter Degraves, and, later, his sons, Charles and John.

The original product lines of beer, ale and porter have been extended to include cider,

CASCADE BREWERY
1824 1927

CASCADE BREWER
EST. 1824

▲
Tooth's Brewery in Hampden Road, Hobart, later became a hat factory and offices

▲▲▶
Substantial hotels developed in the mid-19th century included this one at Fingal

▲▶
Lyall's Brewery operated in King Street, Westbury

◀◀
Cascade brewery at the foothills of Mt Wellington

◀◀
A carved Tasmanian tiger atop Cascade 's former aerated water department

blackcurrant juice and softdrinks. The aerated water department used to be in Cascade's premises in Collins Street, a feature of which is a wooden barrel topped by a carved Tasmanian tiger above the entrance. The tiger is a symbol of Tasmania - just like Cascade and its products.

Across the road from the brewery is "Woodstock", a company-owned homestead that began life in the 1820s as two cottages. Surrounded by impressive gardens, including old plantations of rhododendrons, it became the home of successive general managers until the 1980s and is now used mainly for corporate and private functions.

Boags Brewery was started in 1879 as the Esk Brewery, situated by the banks of the Esk River. It was bought by Messrs James Boag and his sons in 1881, with successive generations of the family being involved in the business. It became part of the Cascade Group in 1922.

The growing of hops has been ongoing in Tasmania but grape-growing has had a more chequered career. The first attempt was in the 1820s when Mr Broughton planted vines at "Prospect", New Town. He was selling his wine by 1827, Captain Charles Swanston undertaking similar endeavours with wine and liquers in 1848. Another pioneer, Dr Matthias Gaunt, started a vineyard in the 1840s at Windermere, by the Tamar River. Dr Gaunt's grave is in the cemetery of picturesque St Matthias' Church, Windermere, which he had built in 1842.

One of the most notorious episodes in the history of Tasmanian viticulture occurred on Maria Island, where Signor Diego Bernacchi planted thousands of vines in the 1880s. During a visit by a parliamentary party in 1886 he sought to impress the visitors by tying additional bunches of grapes to the vines with silk thread. However the deception was revealed when a keen-eyed guest noticed the thread during a grape-cutting ceremony.

The recent history of grape-growing and winemaking dates back to 1956 when Jean Miguet established a vineyard in northern Tasmania near Lalla. He was followed four years later by Claudio Alcorso, who was responsible for the development of Tasmania's first large-scale commercial vineyard, at the Moorilla Estate, Berriedale, on Hobart's northern outskirts. Other pioneers included

◀ *St Matthias' Church, Windermere, built for pioneer vigneron Dr Matthias Gaunt*

brothers David and Andrew Pirie, who started the Pipers Brook Vineyard near Pipers River, in the North-East, in 1975, and a syndicate that established the adjoining Heemskerk Vineyard in 1976.

In the past decade or so Tasmania has achieved international recognition for its wines, especially white wines. Production is aimed at quality rather than quantity, with key centres at Pipers River and the Tamar Valley, in the North, on the east Coast, and in the South at Berriedale, the Coal River Valley and the Derwent Valley.

"Pickings" of another kind that are particularly important to the Tasmanian economy are the potatoes, green peas, onions, French and runner beans and other vegetables that are grown for processing and the fresh food market. The North-West, with its rich basaltic soils, is the main production area as well as being the base for two major processors. Exports from the region today are vastly different from those of the early 19th century when thousands of tons of grey peas were exported to England for use as pigeon feed!

In addition to fostering vegetable-growing and other traditional industries, Tasmania's moderate climate and relative lack of pollution are also proving conducive to the development of new pursuits such as aquaculture. Oysters, scallops, abalone, Atlantic salmon and sea-run trout are among the products of aquaculture research and farming. In the case of Angasi oysters, which resemble European flat oysters, it is like turning back the clock. They are native to the D'Entrecasteaux Channel area and were one of the shellfish eaten by Tasmanian Aborigines. Angasi oysters are being cultivated commercially, along with Pacific oysters, which are farmed in various parts of the State.

Atlantic salmon ova imported in 1984 by the Tasmanian Department of Sea Fisheries formed the basis for a burgeoning industry involving the farming of Atlantic salmon, as well as sea-run trout. Fingerlings from a hatchery at Wayatinah are supplied to fish farms in southern and western Tasmania. By the end of 1989 there were 35 such farms, but several have now amalgamated.

Despite the infancy of the industry, the value of aquaculture products is approaching that of the total figure for wild fish and shellfish takings.

One of the oldest large-scale business activities on the island involves the procuring of timber. Aborigines used to make shelters of split and broken boughs, and timber was a prime building material in settlements established by white settlers.

Sawpits for cutting timber were later replaced with steam-powered mills. There were about a dozen mills in 1854, this number increasing to approximately 250 by 1933.

Raminea's huge sawmill near the Esperance River was the last of the steam-driven mills. It burnt down in 1974 after nearly 100 years' service.

Tasmania has a larger variety of timber than any other temperate country of similar size. Last century, the products of its forests were exported far and wide. Railway sleepers went to China, India and Germany, paving blocks and wharf piles were exported to England and other timber was used for building dykes in Holland. Closer to home, it formed part of Melbourne's docks and provided fuel for the mines of western Tasmania.

In bygone times, one of the main eucalypts, Tasmanian blue gum, which is the strongest and most durable of the southern hardwoods, was unequalled for piling, sleepers and wharf decking, while swamp gum was used for palings, shingles and laths. Stringybark proved ideal for heavy construction purposes and for furniture-making. Blackwood, an ornamental timber that is most prevalent in the North-West, especially around Smithton, was transformed, in particular, into furniture, and Tasmanian myrtle (or beech) was utilised in tramway rails, the bodies of carriages and furniture. Huon pine from the West and South-West was a prized boat-building material.

Macquarie Harbour, on the west coast, became an important base for timber gathering and shipbuilding. It was common to find Huon pines of more than 2 metres in diameter and growing up to 20 metres, while celery-top pine of similar heights and myrtle were also plentiful around the harbour.

Pining sites were established at various points along the lower Gordon River, with a renewed demand for Huon pine in the 1930s encouraging contractors to move upstream. Timber logged from as far as the Olga River was floated in rafts down to the port of Strahan, where two currently operative sawmills include one on the waterfront that still uses the boom and derrick that formerly lifted the rafted Huon pine logs out of the water on to the skidway.

In most parts of the State, extensive tramline systems were built to transport logs from the bush to the sea, where they were loaded on to trading ships. Remains of tramline tracks used in carrying logs from the bush to ports can be seen from Corinna, in the West, to Mole Creek in the North, Bruny Island and Cockle Creek in the South, and many places in between.

Forestry is still a major contributor to the Tasmanian economy. The timber is harvested for the building industry, for the manufacture of paper and for pulp, which is exported. Forests cover over 3.5 million hectares of the island, 38% of which is in State forests while 36% is privately owned. Crown land accounts for another 14% and 11% is in Crown reserves.

In recent times, the growth of exotic species has been a centre of developmental forestry work.

Forests cover nearly half Tasmania's land surface, providing areas for conservation of rare plants and animals, recreation and timber-harvesting. Aborigines used timber as a building material long before Europeans established tramways to carry supplies from the bushland. In addition to eucalypts (below), Tasmania has a number of specialty timbers, such as myrtle (left and lower left), blackwood, sassafras and Huon pine.

▶▶
Queenstown, Tasmania's largest mining town

EST
A.D.1892
ZEEHAN
SCHOOL OF MINES
AND
METALLURGY.

EST
A.D.1892
ZEEHAN
SCHOOL OF MINES
AND
METALLURGY.

Small areas of softwoods, notably radiata pine, have been planted in State forests to cater for sawlog and paper production requirements. Most of these plantations are in the Fingal, Scottsdale, Devonport and Burnie districts. Plantations of hardwoods, including the most valuable eucalypts - stringybark, gum-top stringybark (alpine ash) and swamp gum (mountain ash) are more widespread. However, the greatest area of eucalypt plantations are planted with fast-growing shining gum, which is primarily for pulp wood. Harvested areas are regenerated by the Forestry Commission and by companies involved in logging.

Much of the timber produced in native forests is suitable for sawmilling and paper-making. The establishment of a paper mill at Burnie in 1938 represented the first stage of industrial expansion that has also led to the development of plants producing newsprint, building panel-boards, woolpulp and woodchips.

Associated Pulp and Paper Mills Limited, which manufactures paper at Burnie, is of vital importance to the city and is its largest employer. The company, a division of North Broken Hill Limited, also produces particle board and paper at Wesley Vale and has a woodchip plant at Long Reach, in the Tamar Valley.

◀

Zeehan's School of Mines and Metallurgy has been converted into a West Coast Pioneers Memorial Museum, where exhibits include a locomotive that used to travel on the Abt railway between Queenstown and Macquarie Harbour

Australian Newsprint Mills Limited at Boyer, in the Derwent Valley, became Australia's first newsprint mill when it was established on the banks of the River Derwent in 1941. Approximately 60% of Australia's newsprint comes from this plant which, like APPM, is the district's main centre of employment.

At Port Huon, Australian Paper Manufacturers Limited has produced pulp in pelletised form and woodchips for the export market, while Tasmanian Pulp and Forest Holdings, which is a subsidiary of North Broken Hill Limited, has a woodchip mill at Triabunna and Forest Resources operates the second woodchip plant built at Long Reach.

It is estimated that one in seven people in Tasmania derive benefits from the forestry industry, either directly or indirectly.

Mining is also of paramount importance to Tasmania, both in terms of income and as the lifeblood of most western Tasmanian centres. The State has a long history of prospecting and mining, with 21 major ore deposits discovered since 1870.

Two important geological events resulted in the extensive mineralisation of western Tasmania. The first involved a major period of volcanic eruption in the Cambrian period (about 550 million years ago) that led to the development of the Mount Read Volcanic Arc and associated copper, lead, zinc, silver and gold ore deposits at Mt Lyell, Rosebery, Que River, Hellyer and Henty. The second event occurred in the Devonian period (about 340 million years ago) when widespread folding and faulting culiminated in the intrusion of large bodies of granite. These contained the tin and tungsten deposits of Renison Bell, Cleveland, Mt Bischoff and King Island.

Aborigines were the first Tasmanian miners, with stone, Darwin glass and ochre among the substances that were sought. Spongelite quarries in the Arthur River area were a source of cutting material, while Darwin glass from Maydena and Maxwell River districts and stone suited to the manufacture of tools were highly tradeable items. Ochre mines, which were found in many places, notably around Deloraine and Oyster Cove, were often a catalyst in the establishment of ceremonial areas as ochre is an important component of Aboriginal culture. Its use signified social and spiritual status.

Colonial settlers also recognised the potential for mining. In Melville's Van Diemen's Land Annual of 1834 it was stated that *"Van Diemen's Land exhibits abundant proof of being rich in minerals. Iron ore abounds everywhere; and specimens of copper, lead, zinc, and according to some, of the more valuable metals such as silver, platina, and even gold, have been discovered sufficient to place their existence beyond conjecture. Coals have been met in various parts of the colony, although no mines have yet been opened. Limestone is common and of excellent quality. Granite and marble have frequently been dug in small quantities, but no quarries have yet been opened. Near Hobart Town, a fine vein of plumbago, or black lead, was discovered a year or two ago, of very superior quality. In some streams in the interior, handsome crystals have been occasionally found."*

Soon after this report was published coal-mining began on the Tasman Peninsula, at Adventure Bay, Schouten Island and the Denison River. At Bicheno, which was the port for shipment of Denison River coal, it is still possible to see iron rings set into rocks that were used in warping coal boats into the tiny harbour at The Gulch.

Payable gold was found in the Fingal Valley in 1852, followed by important strikes near George Town and north of Mt Arthur and Lilydale. However, the first major period of mineral discoveries didn't start until 1871. A 27-year mineral boom began with the discovery of tin at Mount Bischoff by James "Philosopher" Smith and continued as other important ore bodies were found at places such as Mt Lyell (gold and copper), Zeehan (silver and lead) and Renison Bell (tin).

The township of Waratah developed to service the rich Mount Bischoff Mine, which was worked for 50 years. Meanwhile, tin was also being mined in north-eastern Tasmania. During the heyday of mining around Gladstone, Derby, Weldborough and Ringarooma, between 1876 and 1929, hundreds of Chinese people were among those seeking their fortunes. They generally retained their own culture and lifestyle, and often brought valuable possessions with them. Displays in the Queen Victoria Museum and Art Gallery, Launceston, include an extensively gilded joss house that was presented by some of the Chinese families who lived in the North-East. A Tin Mine Centre at

Aspects of historic north-eastern Tasmanian mining life are portrayed in a Tin Mine Centre at Derby (left) and in the Queen Victoria Museum and Art Gallery, Launceston, where ornately dressed Chinese figures form part of a display centred on a Chinese joss house used by miners

Derby, with a recreated shanty town, an old schoolhouse and mine workings also gives an indication of what life was like when the Briseis Mine was at its peak.

Other significant mining operations in northern Tasmania included the Beaconsfield Gold Mine, which yielded about $7 million worth of gold from depths of up to 450 metres before seepage problems led to its closure in 1914. Details of the mining technology and equipment are outlined in a Grubb Shaft Museum, which is within the ruins of the original mine building. Recently, extensive work has been undertaken to determine whether it is feasible to re-open the Hart Shaft for further mining.

The boom-and-bust history of mining is graphically illustrated on the west coast, where Queenstown and Zeehan have ridden out the "highs" and "lows" for more than a century. The economy of Queenstown is largely dependent on the activities of the Mt Lyell Mining and Railway Company, which is continuing developmental work aimed at extending the life of the Mt Lyell copper mine. Zeehan's population of 10,000 at the height of the silver boom early this century dwindled to about 400 in the 1960s, but then surged again when Renison Limited developed a tin mine at nearby Renison Bell. While the fortunes of Renison are linked with world tin prices, those of Zeehan are bound with this and other companies that are able to exploit the resources of the region.

Copper, gold, lead, zinc and silver are found at Rosebery, where there are the remnants of an aerial ropeway built in 1929 to carry ore in buckets from the Hercules Mine at Williamsford to the Rosebery crusher and separator plant. The ropeway, which was decommissioned in 1985, could carry a total of 197 buckets during the one-hour trip.

Strahan owes its importance to its position as the main port of western Tasmania. The Abt railway, built in 1896 between Queenstown and Macquarie Harbour to carry output from Mt Lyell, operated until 1963. In the early days, copper concentrate and pyrite were taken to Strahan, with coke for the smelters and general supplies being carried on the return trip. Farther north, the formation of the Emu Bay Railway Company in 1897 and its subsequent acquisition of a line built originally by the Van Diemen's Land Company as a horse tram opened up communication between the North-West and previously isolated west coast communities. The track was converted to a railway in 1884, initially servicing Waratah and the Mount Bischoff Mine, with a connection to the nearby Magnet silver mine.

The line was extended in 1900 to link Zeehan with Burnie, marking Burnie's emergence from its wholly farming and forestry-based state. The Emu Bay Raiway, which is a subsidiary of Pasminco Mining, is the only privately owned railway in Tasmania. Its expansion continued in 1989 when a 12-kilometre rail spur was built from the mainline track to enable zinc-lead-silver concentrates from Aberfoyle's Hellyer Mine to be transported direct to Burnie.

The discovery of the Hellyer base metals deposit in 1983 formed part of the modern period of mineral exploration and mine development. Between 1965 and 1991 tungsten was found at Bold Head and Kara, lead-zinc-silver and gold were also discovered at Que River, plus tin at Severn, silica at Corinna and gold at Henty. Additional ore reserves were found during the same period at Savage River (iron ore), Renison, Mt Lyell and the now-decommissioned Cleveland tin mine.

Tasmania's major mines and its mineral processing plants generate half of the State's exports - as well as continuing the traditions established by the pioneer miners who laboured in a rudimentary fashion without knowledge of the state-of-the-art geophysical and geochemical techniques used by today's explorers.

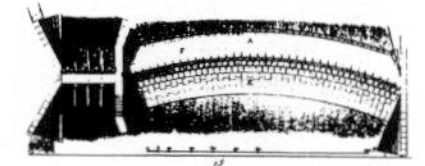

All Tasmanians are now aware of the multiplicity of uses of electric power but it was a different situation in 1893 when Hobart was the first Australian capital city with an electric tramway system. The original double-deckers of Hobart and Launceston later gave way to single-deck trams, with trolley buses, which ran on overhead wires, joining the public transport network in 1935. Trams and trolley buses were both phased out by 1968, when motor buses took over the routes. The Tasmanian Transport Museum at Glenorchy has many examples of modes of transport used around the State.

The initial hydro plant was opened at Duck Reach in 1895, with Launceston subsequently becoming the first city in the southern hemisphere to be connected with electric light. Electricity was a novelty for several decades to come, but by 1937 it was reported that Queenstown used electricity more extensively than anywhere else in the Commonwealth... *"Practically every home is equipped with the latest electrical appliances for lightening the drudgery of housework."* Home owners were assisted by the Mt Lyell Mining and Railway Company, which introduced an instalment plan for the purchase of electrical equipment.

The establishment in 1911 of the Hydro-Electric Power and Metallurgical Company, which built a small dam at Great Lake to carry water to Waddamana, was an auspicious event for Tasmania. It heralded the start of an era when the development of power stations for generating electricity would change the face of Tasmanian industry and commerce. This company was taken over in 1914 by the State Government, which formed a Hydro-Electric Department and proceeded to complete the Great Lake scheme.

At the same time, a concerted effort was made to encourage industries using large amounts of energy to establish in Tasmania. The attraction of cheap power rates, plentiful water supplies, ready availability of labour and waterfront factory sites led to the formation in 1917 of the Electrolytic Zinc Company of Australasia's plant at Risdon and a factory of Carbide and Electro Products Limited at Electrona. Now owned by Pasminco Metals-EZ, the Risdon operation is the second largest electrolytic zinc plant in the world, while the carbide works were converted in the 1980s for the production of silicon.

The drawcard of the cheapest power rates in the Commonwealth was also instrumental in the development of industries such as the Goliath Portland Cement Company Limited, which has been producing cement at Railton since 1928, titanium pigment manufacturer Tioxide Australia Proprietary Limited, which began in Burnie as Australian Titan Products in 1937, Australian Pulp and Paper Mills' Burnie plant, established in 1938, and Cadbury Schweppes Australia Limited, whose cocoa and confectionary factory at Claremont dates back to the 1920s. Australia's first aluminium smelter, now operated by Comalco Aluminium (Bell Bay) Limited, was established in 1955 at Bell Bay, which is also the base for Tasmanian Electro-Metallurgical Company Proprietary Limited, a major alloy manufacturer.

In 1930, the Hydro-Electric Department became the Hydro-Electric Commission, a statutory authority, and for more than 40 years Tasmania was the only Australian State with an electric power system based almost entirely on hydro installations. The situation changed in 1971 when an oil-fired thermal station came on line at Bell Bay. Nowadays, this station is among 27 power stations in operation on the Tasmanian mainland, the latest developmental project involving the King River and Anthony schemes on the west coast.

A hallmark of Tasmanian industry and commerce is the number of operations that have been carried on by successive generations of families. It is particularly noticeable in the printing and publishing industries, with the State's three daily newspapers all having had major periods of domination by one family. In the case of "The Advocate", it has been owned by the Harris family since 1890, when it was published as the "Wellington Times." Tasmania's oldest newspaper, "The Examiner", which was first produced in 1842, was controlled by the Rolph family for nearly a century, and "The Mercury", dating back to 1854 when "The Guardian" was acquired by John Davies, who renamed it the "Hobarton Mercury", remained in the control of the Davies family for a similar length of time.

One of the earliest businesses that is still operative is J. Walch and Sons Proprietary Limited, of Macquarie Street, Hobart. The firm began as Tegg's publishers, printers and manufacturing stationers at Wellington Bridge, Hobart, in 1836. By 1859, when the following advertisement appeared in "Davies's Tasmanian Almanack and General Intelligencer", Walch's also had an outlet in Brisbane Street, Launceston:

"Messrs J. Walch and Sons can refer with confidence to the arrangements they have made in London for the

SAVINGS BANK

regular supply of the latest publications from the principal Houses in the Book Trade - arrangements which, they trust, will enable them to keep the shelves in both their Establishments well supplied with Standard and Popular Literature, from which selections can at all times be made to gratify the taste of the approved reader."

Walch's own products have included annual Tasmanian almanacs produced from 1863 to 1980, which were generally referred to as "the red books" and contained information about the people and activities of State and local governments.

Tasmania's banking history has been somewhat more turbulent than that of many long-running commercial enterprises. The SBT Bank, which changed its name to the Trust Bank following its acquisition of the Tasmania Bank in 1991, proved an exception. The SBT, known originally as the Hobart Savings Bank, was founded in 1845 by philanthropist and store keeper George Washington Walker. It has come a long way since it opened in Walker's drapery shop in Liverpool Street with the object of encouraging "frugality, prudence, and industry in the community, and more particularly to enable the working classes to improve their circumstances, by means easily within their reach." The equivalent of 10 cents was all that was required to open an account.

Economic panic resulted from the collapse in 1891 of the Bank of Van Diemen's Land, which was founded in 1823 and had its first premises on the site now occupied by the Australian Stock Exchange in Macquarie Street. The collapse was due to overtrading in securities of insufficient value. When the bank went into liquidation,George Adams, of Tattersalls, arranged a lottery to dispose of the assets. The prizes listed in a grand lottery brochure of 1894 included:

1st - A magnificent corner property in the centre of the city of Hobart (on the corner of Murray and Liverpool Streets). Total value £26,000

2nd -A central hotel property (Hadley's Orient Hotel, Murray Street). Value £22,500

7th - Bank premises in St John Street, Launc eston. Value £8,000

13th-Bank premises, Devonport (recently completed). Value £5,000

24th-Royaal (sic) Exchange Hotel, Zeehan. Value £2,500

Hadley's Hotel continues to survive as a Hobart institution. "The Mercury" Pictorial Annual of 1936 urged people to *"rendezvous any hour of the day - any afternoon for tea or cocktails - you'll find the lounges, the smoke rooms, cheerful with life and social intercourse. There is none of the confusion, nor studied cordiality of hotels that are merely 'big' - you 'live' at Hadleys, for there - go your friends."*

◀
Leadlighting and solid timber fittings have been retained in the Trust Bank's branch in lower Murray Street, Hobart, which for many years was the head office of the Hobart Savings Bank

NO ESCAPE
NO ESCAPE

The Arts and Leisure

▲
"Studio Still Life" by Jack Carington Smith (From the collection of the Tasmanian Museum and Art Gallery)

◀
Portraits of composers decorate the dome of the Theatre Royal, Hobart

The cultural heritage of Tasmania extends back thousands of years. There is evidence of the rich spiritual and artistic lives of the Aborigines through their paintings and carvings, their melodies and dances. From the beginning of the 19th century aspects of European settlement were often incorporated in the dances, which were frequently based on the behaviour of animals such as kangaroos, emus and, later, dogs and horses.

A festival held in January each year at Oyster Cove is aimed at passing on this heritage to young people of the Aboriginal community and at encouraging white Tasmanians to look beyond the 200-year barrier and make cross-culturalism part of multi-culturalism.

Other annual events with artistic and cultural themes include the Salamanca Arts Festival, Hobart, the Mersey Valley Tasmanian Music Festival, Devonport, and the Circular Head Arts Festival, Stanley.

The unhurried lifestyle in Tasmania, the clear light and the abundance of raw materials that are suitable for working into world-class items as diverse as pottery bread crocks, woven wall hangings and timber furniture and acccessories have long been an inspiration for artists and artisans.

John Glover was the first professional artist of note to settle in Australia. He was already 64 when he emigrated to Tasmania in 1831, the move being motivated by a combination of factors - the attraction of the island's novel landscape, the possibility of obtaining a free land grant and the chance of improving his family's economic situation. He settled initially at "Ring Farm", Tea Tree, but soon moved to a property at Mills Plains on the slopes of Ben Lomond that he named "Patterdale" - after one of his favourite places in Cumberland.

In 1835, the Duke of Orleans, later to become King Louis Phillippe of France, bought two Tasmanian landscapes by Glover. An exhibition that year in London of Glover's English and European landscapes, plus paintings of the Australian landscape, flora and Aborigines, was enthusiastically received. A reviewer for "The Times" newspaper claimed the Australian works *"will convey a more correct idea than the mere reading of books of travel can convey... the country itself is beautiful and picturesque... in some districts magnificent and sublime."*

Glover was a deeply religious man and it is believed that he designed the simple chapel at Deddington, just near "Patterdale." He is buried in the adjoining cemetery.

◀ "My Harvest Home", an oil painted by John Glover in 1835 (From the collection of the Tasmanian Museum and Art Gallery)

▲▲ *Portrait of John Glover by Mary Morton Allport*

▲ *Deddington Chapel, by Glover, is a short distance away from "Patterdale", the property where he lived for most of his time in Tasmania. He is buried in the chapel grounds.*

Other talented free settlers whose artwork provides a valuable record of the 19th century included Benjamin Duterrau, who is remembered, in particular, for his paintings and etchings of Aborigines, John Skinner Prout, an artist on stone, Francis Guillemard Simpkinson (who in 1869 adopted the additional name of de Wesselow), a colonial watercolourist, and Mary Morton Allport, who was the first woman printmaker in the Australian colonies. In 1832 she sought work painting miniatures and in 1845 she was among exhibitors in Hobart Town's earliest exhibition of paintings.

William Charles Piguenit was the first Australian-born landscape artist of European descent. Born in Hobart in 1836, he became a draftsman in the Tasmanian Survey Department and was an avid traveller. Describing a trip to western Lake St Clair in 1873, he said he was *"delighted at the lofty and rugged mountain ranges, deep ravines, great valleys, more or less precipitous, and covered in the greater part with dense forests and impenetrable scrubs."*

Piguenit stipulated in his will that any of his paintings that were not sold at his death should be destroyed. As a result, substantial prices are paid for his remaining works.

Captain Haughton Forrest, who was the police superintendent at Sorell, was a noted marine painter, while portrait-painter Jack Carington Smith, watercolourist Max Angus, teacher-artist Lucien Dechaineux and avante-garde, early Modern artists Edith Holmes, Rosamund McCulloch and Dorothy Stoner are among those who have contributed to the Tasmanian art heritage of the 20th century.

Others who have carved a name for themselves are sculptor Stephen Walker, whose creations in bronze and other materials often feature Tasmanian themes, poets such as Louisa Anne Meredith, Clive Sansom, James McAuley and Gwen Harwood, and author Henry Savery, who wrote Australia's first novel, "Quintus Servinton", published anonymously in 1830 by Henry Melville and,later, in London. Savery's literary works, which also include the first book of essays written and published in this country, "The Hermit of Van Diemen's Land", produced by controversial newspaper proprieter Andrew Bent, are his only monument. A convicted forger who was transported for life in 1825, Savery is buried in an unmarked grave on the Isle of the Dead.

Significant endeavours of another kind were made in the literary field in the 1830s when the "Hobart Town Monthly Magazine" was produced to show *"friends and well-wishers in 'Old England' that Tasmania is not devoid of individuals who have the means, as well as the desire, of cultivating Literature as well as Land, and of devoting their best and liveliest energies to its interests and advancement."*

The first public library was established in 1837 by the Bothwell Literary Society, whose patron was Sir John Franklin. The library operated from a cottage in Alexander Street, which was named after a pioneer settler, Alexander Reid, who is credited with introducing golf to Australia. One of the oldest country libraries is at Evandale, the quaint 1847 timber building having been restored in 1984.

The headquarters of the State Library of Tasmania, on the corner of Murray and Bathurst Streets, Hobart, houses a number of very important historic collections in addition to its books and other reference material. This is the base for the Archives Office of Tasmania, the Tasmaniana Library containing a definitive collection of books published in Tasmania, and the Crowther Library, which has a large research collection of books, pamphlets and other items relating to Tasmania and other parts of Australia. The Crowther material was gathered by Dr. W.E.L.H. Crowther and other members of his family, who came to Tasmania in 1825. The Allport Library and Museum of Fine Arts was established as a result of a bequest from Mr Henry Allport, the great-grandson of pioneers Joseph and Mary Morton Allport, whose family was intimately associated with the development of art in Tasmania. Antique furniture, china, glass, silver, pictures, prints and rare books are among the display items.

A Botanical and Horticultural Society of Van Diemens Land established in 1843 was a forerunner of the Royal Society of Van Diemens Land for Horticulture, Botany and the Advancement of Science. This title was later shortened to the Royal Society of Tasmania, which is now the oldest Royal Society outside Britain

The Society was entrusted with the management of Hobart's Botanical Gardens and, in 1848, members also established a museum of more than 1,500 specimens in a section of the present Parliament House. The Society acquired its own building in 1863, with a special Art Treasures Exhibition held to coincide with the opening of the Tasmanian Museum on the corner of Macquarie and Argyle Streets. The first section of the art gallery was added in 1901.

Today, this complex and the Queen Victoria Museum and Art Gallery, Launceston, are major repositories of artworks and artefacts associated with the State's history.

◀ *Allport Library and Museum of Fine Arts*

Responsibility for the Botanical Gardens passed back to the Crown in 1885 and a Board of Trustees with representatives of the State Government, the Hobart City Council, the Royal Society and the University of Tasmania manages what is now called the Royal Tasmanian Botanical Gardens.

◀ *An "Antipodean Voyage" fountain in the Royal Tasmanian Botanical Gardens was designed and built by Stephen Walker*

They cover a 13.5-hectare site, with buildings including the house of the original superintendent, William Davidson, who was appointed in 1828. He brought about 2,000 vines and fruit trees with him when he came from England and further orders for trees and seeds were placed during his first year in office. In addition, the seeds of 150 native plants were gathered from the slopes and summit of Mt Wellington for planting in the gardens.

Substantial brick boundary walls were built on the instruction of Governor Arthur and, subsequently, Governor Eardley Wilmot. Internal heating in the first wall fostered the growth of exotic fruits and flowers, a traditional English idea that was popular in the early 19th century, while the second structure, which extends 280 metres along what was once the eastern boundary, is believed to be the longest span of a convict-built brick wall still in existence.

A favourite attraction at the gardens, the lily pond, was established in 1848 as a storage dam for water from the adjoining creek, thus eliminating the need for the costly carting of water from the town. The conservatory, regarded as one of the finest in the British Commonwealth, is among other features. It was built in 1939 and materials include stone from the demolished old Hobart General Hospital. An Antipodean Voyage fountain, erected in 1972 to commemorate the 200th anniversary of the first French exploration and scientific discovery in Tasmanian waters, and a Japanese garden are recent additions.

Tasmania's links with Britain are evident in the large number of organisations and establishments that have been granted Royal Charter, but the word "royal" is also incorporated in other titles, such as the Theatre Royal, and in the sport of Royal tennis, which first received royal approval from King Henry V111 in the 16th century.

The Theatre Royal began life in 1837 as the Royal Victoria and it is Australia's oldest surviving theatre. Re-built in 1857, it also underwent massive internal restoration following a fire in 1984. The classic interior includes an auditorium dome decorated with the portraits of 10 composers, a magnificent central chandelier and a sculpted, gilded version of the mythological Greek god of words and pastures, Pan, who has watched over generations of theatregoers from above the stage. More of the theatre's heritage is contained in areas such as The Shades, a 19th century basement tavern that is said to be one of the haunts of Fred the Ghost, a reputed "custodian" of the building!

Hobart's Royal tennis courts were the first of three such establishments in Australia. Built in 1875 behind a stone building fronting Davey Street, they are modelled on courts in Haymarket, London, and have been the venue for many national and international tournaments. The Governor's Cup, initiated in 1975 to commemorate 100 years of Royal tennis in Tasmania, is a world open challenge event.

The north-western township of Latrobe, which was settled in the late 1830s and rose to prominence when it became an important railway terminus during construction of the north-western line 40 years later, has also placed Tasmania on the map for major sporting events. A cycling club formed here in 1890 set the pace for later developments, including Australia's "blue ribbon" cycling carnival, the annual Latrobe Wheel Race, which is the nation's richest handicap cycling event. This was also the setting for the first carnival conducted by the United Australian Axemen's Association, in 1891.

Contrasting with Latrobe's wheel races, international penny farthing championships are staged each year at Evandale, when the town turns back the clock and "bone-shakers" reign supreme on the town's roadways.

In addition to highly organised sporting and cultural events, Tasmania's mountains, waterways, national parks, forest reserves and wilderness areas, lend themselves to the pursuit of recreational activities...

It is the combination of these natural assets and the varied endeavours of the island's inhabitants, both fateful and fortunate, that have shaped the face of today's Tasmania. Hopefully, an understanding and awareness of this heritage will ensure that it is preserved for tomorrow's generations.